M000215196

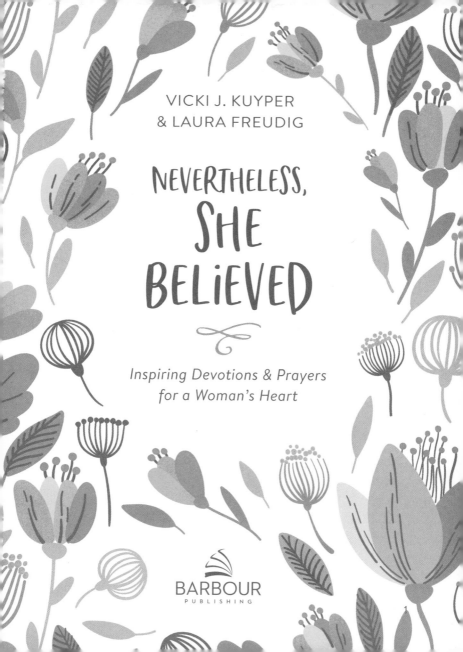

VICKI J. KUYPER
& LAURA FREUDIG

NEVERTHELESS, SHE BELIEVED

*Inspiring Devotions & Prayers
for a Woman's Heart*

BARBOUR
PUBLISHING

Published by Barbour Publishing, Inc., 1810 Barbour Drive, Uhrichsville, Ohio 44683, www.barbourbooks.com

Our mission is to inspire the world with the life-changing message of the Bible.

 Member of the
Evangelical Christian
Publishers Association

Printed in China.

NEVERTHELESS, HAVE FAITH!

Without faith it is impossible to please Him, for he who comes to God must believe that He is, and that He is a rewarder of those who diligently seek Him.

HEBREWS 11:6 NKJV

The Bible says that "without *faith* it is impossible to please God" (Hebrews 11:6 NIV, emphasis added). God places its importance at the very top of the list, and the reason is simple: Faith is the key by which we gain access to Him. How can we love Him when we aren't sure He exists? How can we trust Him when we aren't sure He wants to be part of our lives? By faith we come into God's presence and establish a relationship with Him.

Nevertheless, She Believed was designed to open your eyes to faith, to take it from word to concept to experience. It is our prayer that as you move through these pages, you will hear God's voice calling you to place your faith in Him in every aspect of your life.

GiFTS

*In his grace, God has given us different
gifts for doing certain things well.*
ROMANS 12:6 NLT

You are a unique woman. Your blend of experience, talents, and personality are gifts you can share with the world. But when you choose to put your faith in God, you also receive "spiritual" gifts. God gives you these abilities so you can help others see Him more clearly. By using gifts such as teaching, serving, or encouragement, you make faith visible. Ask God to help you understand and use the gifts He's so graciously given to you.

Lord, we often question how You've made us. Why aren't we good at this? Why do we struggle so much with that? Help us to rest in who we are in Christ, knowing that both our struggles and our gifts are from You, to be used for Your glory. Amen.

No Comparison Necessary

We will not compare ourselves with each other as if one of us were better and another worse. We have far more interesting things to do with our lives. Each of us is an original.
GALATIANS 5:26 MSG

When God created each of us, He wove together a wonderful woman unlike any other. But at times it's tempting to gauge how well we're doing by using other women as a measuring stick. Faith offers a different standard. The Bible encourages us to use our abilities in ways that honor God. Some abilities may take center stage, while others work quietly in the background. Just do what you can with what you have in ways that make God smile. No comparison necessary.

God, when I see another woman with gifts that I wish I had, help me turn my envy into praise. Thank You for her. Thank You for making her a light and inspiration to many. Help me support her in the work You've given her, so that You may be glorified even more. Amen.

FROM GOD'S PERSPECTIVE

*Has not God chosen those who are poor in the eyes
of the world to be rich in faith and to inherit the
kingdom he promised those who love him?*

JAMES 2:5 NIV

Being rich in faith is the secret to leading an abundant life. That's because faith allows us to see life from God's perspective. We begin to appreciate how much we have instead of focusing on what we think we lack. We understand that what's of eternal worth is more valuable than our net worth. We feel rich, regardless of how much, or how little, we own. True abundance flows from the inside out—from God's hand straight to our hearts.

---

*Dear Father, we are blessed beyond measure—both now
and in eternity—because You have given us the immeasurable
gift of Your only Son, Jesus Christ. Help us to keep our
eyes fixed on that treasure, which will never fade
and cannot be taken from us. Amen.*

EXCEEDED EXPECTATIONS

"I have come that they may have life,
and that they may have it more abundantly."
JOHN 10:10 NKJV

In Jesus' day, the people of Israel were looking for the Messiah promised in scripture. They believed this Savior would restore Israel to its former power and prosperity. Jesus didn't meet their expectations—He exceeded them. Jesus offered them an abundance of riches that couldn't be stolen or decrease in value—true treasures like joy, peace, forgiveness, and eternal life. Jesus offers these same treasures to you. All you need do is place your faith in Him.

We want what You want, Lord. We want to desire the things You desire. Forgive us for being goaded and deceived by the world into wanting the things that it offers. We ask for the Holy Spirit to fill us so we will desire everything that pleases You. Amen.

COMPLETELY!

The Spirit makes us sure that God will
accept us because of our faith in Christ.
GALATIANS 5:5 CEV

God accepts you completely. You don't need to clean up your language, change your lifestyle, or step inside of a church. Once you put your faith in Jesus, things between you and God are made right. Period. But acceptance is only the first step in this relationship. As God's Spirit continues working in your heart, He gives you the desire and strength you need to mature into who you were created to be—an amazing woman whose character reflects God's.

Dear Lord, we praise You that because of the perfect sacrifice
of Jesus, we are acceptable to You in any condition: even when
we're broken, weary, filthy, crooked. We praise You that
You don't discard us or dismiss us as worthless. Instead,
You make us new. In praise and thanksgiving, amen.

LOVING ACCEPTANCE

Accept other believers who are weak in faith, and don't argue
with them about what they think is right or wrong.
ROMANS 14:1 NLT

Talking about faith can get tricky at times. What you believe and how faith plays a part in your everyday life may differ from those around you—even from those who attend the same church. Faith is important. But so is love and acceptance. God wholeheartedly accepts each and every one of His children and asks that we do the same. Listen in love. Learning to accept others the way Jesus did is more important than always seeing eye-to-eye.

Gracious Lord, I am not like You. I judge; I jump to
conclusions; I parcel out my love based on correct
performance. Forgive me, Father. I need Your Spirit
to help me reach out in love to those around
me, as we all walk toward You. Amen.

CELEBRATE!

We remember before our God and Father your work produced by faith, your labor prompted by love, and your endurance inspired by hope in our Lord Jesus Christ.
1 THESSALONIANS 1:3 NIV

When you work hard toward completing a goal, accomplishing what you've set out to do is something worth celebrating. When your accomplishment is fueled by faith, you can be certain you'll never celebrate alone. God sees the time, energy, and heart you put into your work. Better yet, He adds His own power to your efforts. This means that with God, you can accomplish things you could never do solely on your own. That's something truly worth celebrating—with God!

Lord, thank You for blessing the work of my hands. Thank You for the plans You have for my future. . .plans to prosper me and not to harm me. I know I can trust You to carry them to completion. I look forward—with joy!— to what You will do! Amen.

COURAGEOUS FOOTSTEPS

*"Blessed is she who has believed that the
Lord would fulfill his promises to her!"*
LUKE 1:45 NIV

In Jesus' day, women had fewer opportunities to stretch their wings creatively and professionally than they do today. That didn't stop them from holding tightly to God's promises and stepping out to act on what they believed. You can follow in their courageous footsteps. Whatever you believe God wants you to do, big or small, don't hold back. Today, take at least one step toward your goal. With God's help, you'll accomplish everything He's set out for you to do.

---

*Dear Lord, sometimes I'm afraid to keep walking
toward the goals You have planted in my heart. The way
seems long and hard. . .and I am still so far from where I long
to be. Yet I know that You are with me. Help me take
a step forward in faith today. Amen.*

OVERFLOWING WITH HOPE

We live by faith, not by sight.
2 CORINTHIANS 5:7 NIV

Faith changes how we see the world. From all appearances, your circumstances may seem daunting. Your opportunities limited. Your future set in stone. But when you place your faith in God instead of what you see, your heart can't help but overflow with hope. God's power is at work behind the scenes. He's working in both you and your circumstances. He promises to bring something good out of every situation, no matter how things may look on the outside.

Father, I am so grateful that I don't have to judge based on appearances—You look past appearances and so can I. No matter how dark the way seems or how weak and weary I feel, I know that You are—right now—working all things for good. With praise, amen.

CLOTHE YOUR HEART

What matters is not your outer appearance—
the styling of your hair, the jewelry you wear,
the cut of your clothes—but your inner disposition.
1 PETER 3:3–4 MSG

For many women, getting dressed is a bit like painting a portrait. They put themselves together in a way that reflects how they want others to see them. Successful? Confident? Youthful? A bit of a rebel? Who you are on the inside speaks much louder than what you wear on the outside. As you allow God, through faith, to clothe your heart in love and compassion, you'll automatically become more attractive. You'll draw others toward you and God, regardless of what you are wearing.

Dear Lord, thank You for reminding us that what we look like is not who we are. You see the inside, where it counts. Help us to hold lightly the things which will fade and to work at making truly beautiful the things that will last forever. Amen.

SPIRITUAL ARSENAL

*Put on all the armor that God gives, so you can
defend yourself against the devil's tricks.*
EPHESIANS 6:11 CEV

A woman donning armor brings to mind images of Xena the
Warrior Princess or Joan of Arc. But the armor God offers is
neither fantasy nor outdated. It's a spiritual arsenal of offensive and defensive gear. It's comprised of weapons such as
truth, righteousness, peace, and faith. There's a battle going
on every day for your mind and heart. But there's no reason
to be afraid. Through faith, God's given you everything you
need to be victorious.

---

*Lord, thank You for the reminder that my only offensive
weapon is Your Word. Forgive me for treating it lightly, for
pushing it aside in favor of more urgent (to my mind) things.
Nothing is more urgent than preparing for the battle You tell
me I am already in. Help me take up my "sword" daily. Amen.*

LiKE A SHiELD

Let your faith be like a shield.
EPHESIANS 6:16 CEV

Some women keep their faith tucked away like a family heirloom, displaying it only on holidays like Easter and Christmas. But if you truly believe what God says is true, faith will be part of your everyday life. Faith is more than words of comfort; it's a shield that can protect you from an assault of doubt or the temptation to do something you know goes against what God has planned for you. Take faith with you wherever you go.

Dear Lord, faith that is not used will weaken. It cannot be saved for later or given to others. It can only be used now. Thank You that our faith in Christ is strong enough to protect us from anything. Help us to strengthen it by leaning on You daily. Amen.

HE DELIVERS

*Faith is confidence in what we hope
for and assurance about what we do not see.*
HEBREWS 11:1 NIV

It's been said that death and taxes are the only things we can be certain of in our lives. The Bible tells us that faith brings its own gift of certainty. Because of God's promises, and His faithfulness in keeping them in the past, we have the assurance that He'll come through for us in the future. He's promised we're loved, forgiven, cared for, and destined for heaven. Rest in the fact that what God promises, He delivers.

---

*Lord, it is a miracle that, through faith, the unseen
becomes more real and dear than what we can touch.
We haven't seen You, yet we love You and believe in You
with our whole heart. Thank You for that inexpressible
joy. . .the certainty of our salvation. Amen.*

SECRET INGREDIENT

This is the secret: Christ lives in you.
This gives you assurance of sharing his glory.
COLOSSIANS 1:27 NLT

When it comes to family recipes, women often remain mum on the secret ingredient that makes their great-grandmother's pot roast, pound cake, or pickled beets stand out from the rest. You have a secret ingredient in your life that assures your future will turn out perfectly. But this secret—that once you put your faith in Jesus, you are assured of spending eternity with Him—is meant for sharing. Pass it on, and you'll be blessing future generations!

Lord, we are the aroma of Christ to a starving world!
We praise You for Your amazing grace. We have no aroma
or flavor on our own that would attract anyone—but through
You, we partake of that divine goodness and others
are drawn in. Praise the Lord! Amen.

DRAWN TOWARD JESUS

Have the same mindset as Christ Jesus: Who, being in very nature God, did not consider equality with God something to be used to his own advantage.

PHILIPPIANS 2:5–6 NIV

Even those who don't believe Jesus is God can agree that He was an extraordinary person. The way Jesus selflessly loved others, reaching out to people who society had cast aside— including women—demonstrates an attitude of compassion, humility, and service. We're drawn to those who sincerely care for us. That's one reason why we're drawn toward Jesus. Believing in a God who believes in us doesn't feel risky; it feels like accepting a free invitation to be unconditionally loved.

Dear Lord, thank You for loving us so much that You would send Your only Son to die for our sins. Help us to be more like You to the people around us. Help us to love, to welcome, to serve. Help us to offer both truth and grace in Your precious name. Amen.

BALANCE

Let the Spirit renew your thoughts and attitudes. Put on your new nature, created to be like God—truly righteous and holy.
EPHESIANS 4:23–24 NLT

Women are notorious for having moods that shift at the slightest provocation. We may blame it on hormones, stress, or the demands of those around us. Regardless of what pushes our mood swings to an all-time high, the truth is we all need an attitude adjustment now and then. Faith provides exactly what we require. As we turn to God in prayer, His Spirit makes us more like Him. He balances our lives and emotions with His power and perspective.

Dear Father, I desperately need Your renewal today. Forgive me for how I have lashed out at those around me; forgive me for how I have forgotten to put on the mind of Christ. Thank You for Your Spirit, pointing out my weaknesses and reminding me of Christ's sufficiency. Amen.

FAiTH THAT WON'T FAiL

*If Christ wasn't raised to life,
our message is worthless, and so is your faith.*
1 CORINTHIANS 15:14 CEV

Faith, in and of itself, is nothing more than trust. If you place your trust in something that isn't trustworthy, your faith is futile. You can have faith that money grows on trees, but ultimately that faith isn't going to help you pay your bills. Putting your faith in Jesus is different. Historical and biblical eyewitness accounts back up Jesus' claims. That means putting your faith in Jesus is both logical and powerful. It's a faith that won't fail.

*Lord, we thank You for being the God who both walked on
mountains and moves them still. Thank You for being the
God who spoke in the past and speaks even today.
Thank You for being trustworthy and true. We place our
hope in You—both now and in the days to come. Amen.*

HEART CHANGES

*Jesus went to Galilee preaching the Message of
God: "Time's up! God's kingdom is here.
Change your life and believe the Message."*
MARK 1:14–15 MSG

What you believe will influence the choices you make. If you believe in gravity, you won't jump from a seventh story balcony to save time in getting to your hair appointment. If you believe what Jesus says, you'll change the way you live. Jesus often talks about the importance of traits such as honesty, purity, and generosity. Though God's Spirit helps change your heart, it's the daily choices you make that help bring traits like these to maturity.

---

*Lord, help me to trust that my obedience is bearing
fruit even when it feels like nothing is really changing.
Help me to keep believing that You are working in and
through me. Help me to see—without knowing the
ending—that You are writing my story. Amen.*

LiFE LETTER

*These are written so that you will put your faith in
Jesus as the Messiah and the Son of God. If you
have faith in him, you will have true life.*
JOHN 20:31 CEV

The Bible is like a letter from your best friend. In it, God shares
how much He loves you, what He's been up to since the
creation of the world, and His plans for the future. You're an
important part of those plans. The life you live through faith
is the letter you write in return. But others will also sneak a
peek at your "life letter." The life you live may be the only Bible
some people ever read.

---

*Lord, I want my life to be a living representation of the
Gospel—to live with visible repentance and joy. But often I am
afraid to speak the truth. Help me to be discontent
with simply showing; help me tell. For how will
others know if they have not heard? Amen.*

INTO PRACTICE

Truth, righteousness, peace, faith, and salvation are more than words. Learn how to apply them. You'll need them throughout your life. God's Word is an indispensable weapon.
EPHESIANS 6:14–17 MSG

What you do with God's words is ultimately what you decide to do with God. If you read the Bible for inspiration, without application, your faith will never be more than a heartwarming pastime. While it's true the Bible can be a source of comfort, it's also a source of power and an instrument of change. Invite God's Spirit to sear the Bible's words into your heart. Then step out in faith and put what you've learned into practice.

Dear Lord, we want to be doers of the Word, not hearers only. But so often we are content with a lukewarm, passive faith that shies away from engagement. Forgive us, and show us how Your Spirit working in us can turn truth, righteousness, peace, faith, and salvation into actions. Amen.

BELIEVING WITHOUT SEEING

Jesus said, "So, you believe because you've seen with your own eyes. Even better blessings are in store for those who believe without seeing."
JOHN 20:29 MSG

If you're searching for a pair of shoes, you don't rely on a salesperson's description. You want to see them. Try them on. Walk around in them awhile. The same is true when it comes to trying on faith for size. We long to see the One we've chosen to place our faith in. But Jesus says believing without seeing holds its own special reward. Ask Jesus to help you better understand those blessings as you walk in faith today.

Lord, we know we won't really "see" until we see You face-to-face. The waiting is hard sometimes; our eyes strain to see through this dim glass. But we praise You that our faith grows in the waiting, and You are becoming more real, true, and beautiful all the time. Amen.

"NOWHERE" BLESSINGS

"Turn to face God so he can wipe away your sins, pour out showers of blessing to refresh you, and send you the Messiah he prepared for you, namely, Jesus."
ACTS 3:19–20 MSG

Blessings are gifts straight from God's hand. Some of them are tangible, like the gift of a chance acquaintance leading to a job offer that winds up helping to pay the bills. Some are less concrete. They may come wrapped in things like faith, joy, clarity, and contentment appearing seemingly out of "nowhere" amid difficult circumstances. The more frequently you thank God for His blessings, the more aware you'll be of how many more there are to thank Him for.

Dear Lord, help me to continually turn toward You. Your Word says that when I do, You will wipe away my sins and pour out showers of blessings to refresh me. Thank You for enabling me to turn back to You, over and over again. Amen.

PERSONAL TRAINER

Give your burdens to the LORD, and he will take care of you.
He will not permit the godly to slip and fall.
PSALM 55:22 NLT

It's important for us women to do some heavy lifting as we age. Weight-bearing exercise helps keep our bones strong and our muscles toned. But bearing mental and emotional weight is another story. These don't build us up. They break us down. Allow faith to become your personal trainer when it comes to what's weighing heavily on your mind and heart. God knows how much weight you can bear. Invite Him to carry what you cannot.

Dear Father, You know the weights of worry, care, trouble,
and trial that I cannot carry on my own; and You know how
often I try to take those burdens out of Your loving hands.
Help me to place them in Your arms over and
over again, where they belong. Amen.

WORRIES INTO PRAYERS

Don't fret or worry. Instead of worrying, pray.
Let petitions and praises shape your worries into
prayers, letting God know your concerns.
PHILIPPIANS 4:6 MSG

Sometimes it feels like it's a woman's job to worry. If you can't be assured that all of your loved ones' physical and emotional needs are being met, fretting about them makes you feel involved—like you're loving them, even if you're powerless to help. But you know Someone who *does* have the power to help. Anytime you feel the weight of worry, whether it's over someone else's problems or your own, let faith relieve you of the burden. Turn your worries into prayers.

Dear God, it is not my nature to turn my worries into prayers,
but I thank You that Your Spirit working in me gives me a
new nature—one that can lift my worries up to You as
many times as they raise their heads. Thank You
for listening to my concerns. Amen.

HEAD-ON

*"If you had faith no larger than a mustard seed,
you could tell this mountain to move from here to there.
And it would. Everything would be possible for you."*
MATTHEW 17:20 CEV

The Bible tells us faith is what moves mountains. Not personal ability. Not perseverance. Not even prayer. These can all play a part in facing a challenge that looks as immovable as a mountain. But it's faith in God's ability, not our own, that's the first step toward meeting a challenge head-on—then conquering it. Remind yourself of what's true about God's loving character and incomparable power. Then move toward the challenge instead of away from it. God's in control.

Lord, You are all-powerful, all-knowing, ever-loving, and always ready to work on our behalf. There is nothing that surprises You, nothing outside of Your control, nothing that You do not understand completely. We praise You for being a God in whom our faith is fully justified. There is none like You. Amen.

OPPORTUNITIES

Anyone who meets a testing challenge head-on and manages to stick it out is mighty fortunate. For such persons loyally in love with God, the reward is life and more life.
JAMES 1:12 MSG

People joke about how women sit around eating bonbons all day. You know firsthand nothing is farther from the truth. You face challenges each and every day. Instead of viewing challenges as negative, faith helps you see them as opportunities for growth. In the same way that strengthening your body is difficult and often uncomfortable, strengthening your faith can be the same way. But the outcome is worth the challenge. A stronger faith results in a more balanced life.

Dear Lord, thank You for helping us run the race in such a way that we will win the prize. You call us—and enable us—to run with perseverance and joy. Thank You, Jesus, for being our delight, our prize, and our sure reward. He who promises is faithful! Amen.

ULTIMATE MAKEOVER

*Don't become so well-adjusted to your culture that you fit
into it without even thinking. Instead, fix your attention
on God. You'll be changed from the inside out.*

ROMANS 12:2 MSG

You're no longer the woman you once were. When you put
your faith in God, you experience the ultimate makeover.
You're totally forgiven. You're empowered to be able to do
whatever God asks. Your old habits lose their grip over you.
But continued growth and change is a joint effort between you
and God. If there's any area in your life that seems resistant
to change, talk to God about it right now—and every morning
until change takes place.

---

*Lord, I praise You that I am not who I once was. I was
condemned; now I am redeemed. I was lost; now I am found.
I was blind; now I can see. The world looks different,
Lord, and sometimes it's painful. Help me fix
my eyes on You, no matter what. Amen.*

"ADIEU!"

"Forget the former things; do not dwell on the past. See, I am doing a new thing! Now it springs up; do you not perceive it?"
ISAIAH 43:18–19 NIV

Change is a combination of embracing and letting go. When you become a mom, you welcome new love and bid "adieu" to some former freedoms. When you put your faith in God, you embrace the guidance of God's Spirit and abandon your old, self-centered agenda. When times get tough, it's tempting to seek comfort by looking to the past. But life only moves in one direction. Forward. Only by letting go of yesterday can you welcome today's opportunities with open arms.

Dear Father, You make all things new. You have made us new through the power of Your Spirit. Thank You for drawing us; thank You for redeeming us; thank You for sanctifying us. Thank You for giving us the power to lay down our sins and pick up our crosses daily. Amen.

TESTING...

Test yourselves and find out if you really are true to your faith.
If you pass the test, you will discover that Christ is living in you.
2 CORINTHIANS 13:5 CEV

As a kid, you took plenty of tests. Your GPA was determined by how your efforts measured up to a set standard. As a woman of faith, it's time for another test: measure your character against the woman God desires you to become. This isn't a test God grades. It's simply a tool to help you know where your faith needs to grow. Best of all, this is a group project. Jesus is working both in you and through you.

Lord, You live in me! If that isn't a reason to shout, sing, and dance, then nothing is! I know I'm not who You want me to be yet; but, praise God, I'm not who I once was. Help me keep my eyes fixed on Jesus—my model, my guide, and my friend. Amen.

PASS IT ON

Each of you is now a new person. You are becoming more and more like your Creator, and you will understand him better.
COLOSSIANS 3:10 CEV

Moms pass on lots of things to their children, like the shape of their nose or color of their eyes. They can also pass on things like speech patterns or lifestyle preferences. That's because when you spend time together, you pick up the habits of those you're with. In the same way, the more time you spend with God, the more your character begins to resemble His. That's a family resemblance worth celebrating.

Dear Father, thank You for the traits in us that are changing to look more like You: patience, kindness, faithfulness, self-control. We know that change only comes through the work of the Spirit in us, and we ask You to fill us daily with Your transforming power. Amen.

AT EASE

By faith Moses' parents hid him for three months after he was born, because they saw he was no ordinary child, and they were not afraid of the king's edict.
HEBREWS 11:23 NIV

No mother's child is "ordinary." Love enables parents to see their children's unique gifts and potential—and instills in them the desire to protect their children at any cost. Your heavenly Father feels the same way about you and your children. When fear for your children's health or happiness threatens your peace of mind, let faith put your mind at ease. God cares for your children in ways that reach far beyond your own abilities.

Dear Father, thank You for watching over our children at all times. Thank You for loving them even more than we do. Thank You for the talents, skills, and abilities You have given them. In Your great mercy, please save, sanctify, guide, and protect them. Amen.

ADVENTUROUS TALES

It's the living—live men, live women—who thank you, just as I'm doing right now. Parents give their children full reports on your faithful ways.
Isaiah 38:19 MSG

"Tell me a story. . . ." If you're a mom, you've probably heard those words time and time again. But have you ever told your children stories about your faith? How you came to believe in God and how He's been faithful to you in the past are a part of your spiritual family history. The next time a child asks for a story, tell him or her a true tale of wonder and adventure. Tell a tale about God and His love.

Dear Lord, You have told a wonderful story through the life of each person who has been saved, and part of Your story is to save our families through our testimony and gospel witness. Please loosen our lips to share with our children the miracles You have done and are doing still. Amen.

LiMiTLESS

LORD, you know the hopes of the helpless.
Surely you will hear their cries and comfort them.
PSALM 10:17 NLT

There's only so much one woman can do. There are limits to your strength, your time, and your capacity to love others well. When you reach the limit of your own abilities, a feeling of helplessness can set in. But being helpless isn't synonymous with being hopeless. God is near. He hears every prayer, every longing, and every sigh. His power, love, and time are limitless. Cry out in faith when you need the comfort of your Father's love.

Lord, we praise You for being a God of love. And not only do You love us, but You are so replete with love that it overflows from us to everyone around us. That's not something we can do in our own strength; when we feel like we can't love any more, You can. Amen.

CHANGED HEARTS

Whatever things were written before were written for our learning, that we through the patience and comfort of the Scriptures might have hope.
ROMANS 15:4 NKJV

Reading how women like us have faced difficult circumstances, yet found peace, power, and purpose through faith can be a source of comfort. Whether the account is about Lazarus's sisters Mary and Martha, the woman caught in adultery, or the Samaritan at the well, these women all found comfort in Christ's words. In turn, we can be comforted by their experience. Just as Christ changed their hearts and lives, His words and His love can do the same for us today.

But, Lord, for us to be changed by Your Word, we have to consume it. Give us a hunger to read it; help us choose what is best over what is merely good. Your Word is life, truth, peace, and wisdom. We need all those things so much. . .we need You, Lord. Amen.

LiFE PRESERVER

Cling to your faith in Christ.
· 1 TIMOTHY 1:19 NLT

If you were shipwrecked, you'd cling to your life preserver in hope of rescue. Faith is your life preserver in this world. It keeps your head above water in life and carries you safely into God's arms after death. But it takes commitment to keep holding on tight. Emotions rise and fall. Circumstances ebb and flow. But God is committed to you. His love and faithfulness never fail. By holding tightly to your faith, you can weather any storm.

Dear Lord, thank You that at the same time I am holding on to You, You are holding on to me. Your arms are strong and tireless, and I can rest in the knowledge that You will never let me go. Help me press into You deeper and cling tighter. Amen.

FOLLOW THROUGH

*By faith the walls of Jericho fell, after the army
had marched around them for seven days.*
HEBREWS 11:30 NIV

In the Bible, God asks people to do some pretty unlikely things. Build an ark. Defeat Jericho by walking around its walls. Battle a giant with a slingshot. But when people are committed to doing what God asks, amazing things happen. What's God asking you to do? Love someone who seems unlovable? Break a bad habit? Forgive? Commit yourself to follow through and do what God asks. Through faith, you'll witness firsthand how the unbelievable can happen.

*Dear Father, You never ask us to do something that You do
not also give us the means to accomplish. All is possible
through Your strength. Help us see not impossibilities
but miraculous possibilities! Walls, giants, and sins
will fall at the sound of Your voice. Amen.*

IN STYLE

*As God's chosen people, holy and dearly loved,
clothe yourselves with compassion, kindness,
humility, gentleness and patience.*

COLOSSIANS 3:12 NIV

Before you the leave the house, chances are you make sure you're appropriately dressed. You don't head out to a business meeting in your PJs, to the grocery store in your swimsuit, or off for a jog in heels. Faith offers you a different kind of wardrobe, one that's appropriate for every occasion. By clothing yourself in compassion, you reflect God's very own style—a style that always looks good on you and compliments everyone you meet.

Lord, those things—compassion, kindness, humility, gentleness, and patience—do not come naturally to me. Forgive me for the judgment, unkindness, impatience, and pride that I so often exhibit instead. I ask Your Spirit to clothe me in godly garments as I venture out into the world. Amen.

DEEPER THAN A MOTHER'S LOVE

"Can a mother forget the baby at her breast and
have no compassion on the child she has borne?
Though she may forget, I will not forget you!"
ISAIAH 49:15 NIV

A mother's love could be considered the epitome of compassion. Mothers selflessly carry a child within their own body for nine months, then nourish the newborn with their own milk. They comfort, wean, clean, and cuddle. And, if the situation arose, most mothers would sacrifice their own lives to save the children they love. Yet God's compassion runs even deeper than a mother's love. His loving care is passionate, powerful, and permanent for those who put their faith in Him.

Dear God, thank You for creating mothers and their tender,
life-giving, and sacrificial love. I trust that nothing You do
is without purpose or thought; and I believe You created
mother-love—in part—to show how much greater
Your love is than anything we can imagine. Amen.

GOD-CONFIDENCE

Forget about self-confidence; it's useless.
Cultivate God-confidence.
1 CORINTHIANS 10:12 MSG

You're a beautiful, gifted woman. God created you that way.
You have countless reasons to be confident in what you do,
who you are, and where you're headed—but those reasons
don't rest on your talents, intelligence, accomplishments, net
worth, or good looks. They rest solely on God and His faithfulness. Living a life of faith means trading self-confidence for
God-confidence. It means holding your head high because you
know you're loved and that God's Spirit is working through you.

---

*Father God, when I despair of my sin, I remember that Jesus
has paid for it all. When I fear death, I remember that Jesus
has overcome it. When I sigh at my limitations, I remember
that You created me. And when I flirt with pride,
I remember that I am Your creation. Amen.*

AWED

The Fear-of-God builds up confidence,
and makes a world safe for your children.
PROVERBS 14:26 MSG

When the Bible talks about the "fear of God" it's more about awe than alarm. Through faith, we catch a glimpse of how powerful God really is and how small we are in comparison. Yet the depth of God's love for us rivals the enormity of His might. Regardless of the troubles that may surround you, or what you see on the evening news, you can be confident that God remains in charge, in control, and deeply in love.

Dear Lord, we stand amazed at Your provision, Your promises, Your protection, and Your peace. There is nothing in this life we need to fear but You. Help us to stand with confidence, awe, reverence, and holy fear on the Rock of our salvation. In praise and thanksgiving, amen.

STUFF

Godliness with contentment is great gain.
1 TIMOTHY 6:6 NIV

There's a bumper sticker that claims, "THE ONE WHO DIES WITH THE MOST TOYS WINS." If God wrote a bumper sticker, it might read, "THE ONE WHO'S CONTENT WITH WHAT SHE HAS TRULY LIVES." As your desire for God grows, your longing for more "stuff" takes a distant backseat. That's because through faith, you begin to understand how rich you truly are. God's gifts are better than anything this world has to offer—filling your heart instead of just your home.

Lord, remind me daily of the living hope You have already given me and of the undefiled, unfading, imperishable inheritance waiting for me in heaven. Those are gifts that make everything the world offers seem cheap and tacky. Only Your gifts will satisfy me now and forever. Amen.

PATH TO CONTENTMENT

"You're blessed when you're content with just who you are—no more, no less. That's the moment you find yourselves proud owners of everything that can't be bought."
MATTHEW 5:5 MSG

Being content with what you have is one thing. Being content with who you are is quite another. This kind of contentment isn't complacency. It doesn't negate the importance of striving for excellence or encouraging growth and change. It means being at peace with the way God designed you and the life He's given you. This kind of contentment is only available in daily doses. Through faith, seek God and His path to contentment each and every morning.

Lord, thank You that contentment isn't having what we want but wanting what we have. And when we accept Jesus Christ as our Savior, Your Word promises that You give us everything we need for life and godliness. Everything. Everything! Remind us daily that what we need is already ours. Amen.

NOTHING TO FEAR

The blood of Jesus gives us courage to enter the most holy place by a new way that leads to life! And this way takes us through the curtain that is Christ himself.

HEBREWS 10:19–20 CEV

Imagine standing before a holy, almighty, and perfect God and being judged for how you've lived your life. Every mistake, poor choice, and moment of rebellion would be exposed. Sounds downright terrifying, doesn't it? But through our faith in Jesus, we have nothing to fear. We stand faultless and forgiven. Through Christ, we can gather the courage to look at ourselves as we really are, faults and all, without shame. Being wholly loved gives us the courage to fully live.

Lord, this is amazing grace, and it is offered to us by no other system, god, or religion. Only through Jesus Christ, whose flesh was torn for our salvation can we be rightly seen, fully known, totally loved, and completely forgiven. We are redeemed! Praise the Lord! Amen.

WHATEVER NEEDS DONE

When I asked for your help,
you answered my prayer and gave me courage.
PSALM 138:3 CEV

Why do you need courage today? To apologize? To forgive? To break an old habit? To discipline a child? To love in the face of rejection? Courage isn't just for times when you're facing grievous danger. Any time you face difficult, unpredictable situations it takes courage to move forward. When you're tempted to turn away from your problems, let faith help you turn toward God. With Him, you'll find the courage you need to do whatever needs to be done.

God, sometimes the things You ask me to do seem too hard.
Forgive me for doubting You. I need to trust that what You call
me to do, You will also equip me to accomplish. I can do
all things through You. Give me the courage to step out
in faith, knowing Your hands are holding me up. Amen.

RiGHT HERE, RiGHT NOW

Better is one day in your courts than a thousand elsewhere.
PSALM 84:10 NIV

It's fun daydreaming about places you'd like to visit, goals you'd like to accomplish, or the woman you hope to mature into—someday. But God's only given you one life. Chances are, you'll have more dreams than you'll have days. Instead of living for "someday," God challenges you to put your heart into today. Whether you're sunning on vacation or scrubbing the kitchen floor, the God of the universe is right here with you. That's something worth celebrating!

Lord, thank You for the dreams and goals You have given me and how they motivate me to persevere. Thank You also for this present moment and how I can become more like You right now. Help me live well in the tension between "already" and "not yet." Amen.

INTO HIS ARMS

*"Love the LORD your God, walk in all his ways,
obey his commands, hold firmly to him, and serve
him with all your heart and all your soul."*
JOSHUA 22:5 NLT

Every walk you take is a series of steps that moves you forward. Each day you live is like a single step, moving you closer to—or farther away—from God. That's why it's good to get your bearings each morning. Through reading the Bible and spending time with God in prayer, you'll know which direction to take as you continue your walk of faith. Day by day, God will guide you straight into His arms.

*Dear Father, thank You for waking me early this morning
to read Your Word. Thank You for the promise of a
beautiful day and the sun streaming in through the
windows. Thank You for these quiet minutes to
draw near to You and reorient my feet. Amen.*

BEHIND THE SCENES

We make our own decisions,
but the LORD alone determines what happens.
PROVERBS 16:33 CEV

From the man you choose to marry to how you style your hair, decisions are part of your daily life. But that doesn't mean you're totally in control. Much of life is out of your hands and solely in God's. That's where faith provides a place of peace. Rest in the knowledge that God is working behind the scenes to bring about good in your life. The best decision you'll ever make is to trust in His love for you.

Lord, we think we are in control of things when our lives are running smoothly. But when the waves grow taller and the wind stronger, when children disobey, when money is tight, and sickness comes, we realize we control nothing. We throw ourselves on Your mercy, where we have always been. Amen.

FREE WILL

I pray that your love will keep on growing and that you will fully know and understand how to make the right choices.
PHILIPPIANS 1:9–10 CEV

Free will is a wonderful gift. It allows you to have a say in the storyline of your life. But there are consequences tied to every decision you make, big or small. That's why making wise decisions is so important. The more you allow your faith to influence the decisions you make, the closer you'll be to living the life God desires for you. Invite God into your decision process. Let your "yes" or "no" be preceded by "amen."

Lord, thank You for this reminder that we know very little of the story You are telling with our lives. We see dimly and incompletely, at best. But we praise You for inviting us to talk to You in prayer. Remind us daily to cling to this heavenly lifeline. Amen.

ROOT OF DESIRE

"Wherever your treasure is,
there the desires of your heart will also be."
MATTHEW 6:21 NLT

What does your heart long for? If you look at the root of every deep desire, you'll find something only God can fill. Love, security, comfort, significance, joy. . .trying to satisfy these desires apart from God can only yield limited success. God is the only One whose love for you will never waver. You're His treasure; and His desire is to spend eternity with you. As your faith grows, so will your desire to treasure Him in return.

Lord, sometimes it takes a work of Your Spirit for us to see the
true roots of our desires. We long for wisdom to desire rightly,
and we long for the bravery to look directly at our
desires and say, "Not my will, but Yours." Help us to
treasure You above all else, Father. Amen.

MOTIVATION

You are no longer ruled by your desires,
but by God's Spirit, who lives in you.
<small>ROMANS 8:9 CEV</small>

In preparing to play a role, an actress asks herself, "What's my character's motivation?" That's because what motivates us moves us. If a character's desire is to be admired, rich, beautiful, or loved, that will influence her decisions and actions. As you allow God to work in and through you, your desires begin to fall in line with His. There's no longer any need to act. You're free to be exactly who God created you to be.

Dear Father, we know nothing of the humility of infinite
perfection rubbing shoulders with sinful humanity, but we
praise You for being willing to live among us and in
us. Give us the desire to know You better and be
more fully conformed to Your image. Amen.

FAITH ON THE MOVE

All the believers devoted themselves to the apostles' teaching,
and to fellowship, and to sharing in meals. . .and to prayer.
ACTS 2:42 NLT

The time we set aside to read the Bible and pray each day is often called "daily devotions." Have you ever considered why? Think about what it means to be devoted to your husband, your kids, or your job. Devotion is the commitment of yourself to something or someone you love. The same is true with spiritual devotion. Your spiritual faith is a commitment to love God. And since the word *love* is a verb, an action word, your devotion to God is faith on the move. Where will faith move you today?

Dear Lord, our faith does not only consist of us sitting in a
chair and reading scripture. It's not just folding our hands
and praying. That is where our faith begins, but that is
not where it ends. Help us to take what we learn
in prayer and turn it into action. Amen.

DEVOTED TO OTHERS

Women who claim to be devoted to God should make themselves attractive by the good things they do.
1 TIMOTHY 2:10 NLT

Our devotion to God leads us to be more devoted to others. That's because God's Spirit is at work in us, encouraging us to do what's right. When we keep our promises, weigh our words, and offer a helping hand with no expectation of reward, we are loving God by loving others. Our faith-filled devotion to God brings out the best in us, while at the same time blessing those around us.

Lord, forgive me for not living out my devotion to You with actions. Forgive me for my laziness, selfishness, and unkindness. Forgive me for giving to others with any thought to my own profit. Help me seek to bless others in all I do, regardless of the cost or the reward. Amen.

TRANSFORMED DOUBTS

*Immediately the father of the child cried out and said
with tears, "Lord, I believe; help my unbelief!"*
MARK 9:24 NKJV

Entrusting friends and family to God's care isn't always easy.
One reason is that as women, we're born caretakers—and we
doubt anyone can care for those we love as well as we do. Faith
assures us that God is the only perfect Caregiver. When we
worry about someone, we're doubting God's love, power, and
plan for that person's life. Bring every doubt and worry to God
in prayer. Then allow Him to transform your doubts into faith.

---

*Dear Lord, You know how my faith rises and falls like the
waves of the sea. Sometimes I trust, but more often I try to
soldier on under my own power. Forgive me for trying to
carry the burdens that only You can. Help me
give those burdens back to You. Amen.*

ERASED!

When you ask for something, you must have faith and not doubt. Anyone who doubts is like an ocean wave tossed around in a storm.
JAMES 1:6 CEV

You wouldn't ask a gardener to trim your hair or a house painter to paint your nails. When you ask someone to do something, you ask only those who you believe can actually do what needs done. God can do anything that's in line with His will. If you pray without expecting God to answer, doubt is derailing your faith. Ask God to help you understand the "whys" behind your doubts. He can help you erase each one.

Dear God, when we truly understand Your power and love, we will no longer doubt. You can do anything! Help me to pray in faith, knowing You are always hearing and answering, even if sometimes Your answer is "no" or "not yet." We rest in that. Amen.

GROWiNG FRiENDSHiP AND FAiTH

*When we get together, I want to encourage you in your faith,
but I also want to be encouraged by yours.*
ROMANS 1:12 NLT

When women get together, there's usually a whole lot of talking going on. Conversing, counseling, giggling, and catching up on the latest news are all wonderful ways to build a friendship. But if you want to build your faith, take time to encourage one another. Tell your friends how you've seen God at work in their lives. Share what God's been teaching you. Ask questions. Pray. Praise. Your friendship will grow right along with your faith.

Dear gracious heavenly Father, thank You so much for my friends. They are truly gifts from You and bring me strength, joy, and wisdom in abundance. Help me to cherish them. Help our friendship to be firmly rooted in Christ so that together we may grow closer to You. Amen.

You're Loved

The humble will see their God at work and be glad.
Let all who seek God's help be encouraged.
PSALM 69:32 NLT

Asking someone for help can be humbling. Even if that someone is a close girlfriend. But if she agrees to assist you and actually comes through for you, you can't help but be encouraged. Knowing someone reached out to you means that person cares. It means you matter. You're loved. Know that God's help means the very same thing. He cares for you because He cares *about* you. Let that fact encourage you in your faith today.

Lord, thank You for our friends who have acted as the hands and feet of Jesus. They are Your instruments in our lives, and we praise You for Your care of us through their ministry. Help us to ask for help as easily as we give it. Amen.

PATH TO HEAVEN

God loved the people of this world so much that he gave his only Son, so that everyone who has faith in him will have eternal life and never really die.

JOHN 3:16 CEV

Eternal life doesn't begin after you die. It begins the day you put your faith in Jesus' love. Right now, you're in the child-hood of eternity. You're learning and growing. Like a toddler trying to master the art of walking, you may wobble a bit at times. But if you fall, God helps get you back on your feet again. Once your faith sets you on the path toward heaven, nothing—absolutely nothing—can prevent you from reaching your destination.

Dear Father in heaven, help us keep walking forward, toward You, until our faith eventually becomes sight in eternity. Forgive us for our wobbles, missteps, and wrong turns. Thank You for helping to keep our eyes fixed on You and the sure promise of eternal life. Amen.

A HAPPY ENDING

*Because you kept on believing, you'll get
what you're looking forward to: total salvation.*
1 PETER 1:9 MSG

Your salvation comes through faith in Christ. The end result of that salvation is eternal life. Though you're not home in heaven yet, that doesn't mean its existence isn't relevant to you right now. Holding on to your hope of heaven gives you an eternal perspective. It frees you from the fear of death, inspires you to tell others about God's everlasting love, and reminds you that no matter what you face in this life, you're guaranteed a happy ending.

*Lord, You are so good. Thank You for the gift of salvation
that was ours the moment we believed! That present
reality and future hope is a gift You offer to everyone,
and we pray that You would give us the strength and
courage to share that gift with others. Amen.*

POWERFUL LESSONS

*Teach believers with your life: by word,
by demeanor, by love, by faith, by integrity.*
1 TIMOTHY 4:12 MSG

As a little girl, perhaps you played "school" before you ever attended class. If you had the coveted role of "teacher," you got to tell your friends what to do. As an adult, you're still playing the role of teacher, whether you're aware of it or not. When what you believe changes the way you live and love, others notice. Who knows? The most powerful lessons you ever teach may be those in which you never say a word.

Lord, without speaking the Word, my demeanor, love, faith, and integrity often just make others think I'm a "good person." Help me to show them, instead, that I am a sinner saved only by grace. Only You are good! Praise the Lord! Amen.

ONE WORTH FOLLOWING

*Follow the example of the correct teaching I gave you,
and let the faith and love of Christ Jesus be your model.*
2 TIMOTHY 1:13 CEV

The Bible's a pretty thick book. It looks like there's a lot to learn. But Jesus said that if we love God and others, we've fulfilled everything written there. How do we do that? Look to Jesus' own life as recorded in the gospels. Jesus never treats people like an interruption or inconvenience. He listens, comforts, and cares. He spends time with His Father in prayer, regardless of His busy schedule. Jesus' example is one worth following.

*Dear Lord, one of the miracles of the Christian life is
that it's simple enough for a child to understand yet
complex enough to keep us thinking, praying, and praising
our entire lives. Help us to reach out to others with
the simple, rich message of the Gospel. Amen.*

A GLIMPSE OF GOD

*In the morning, LORD, you hear my voice; in the morning
I lay my requests before you and wait expectantly.*

PSALM 5:3 NIV

If you're expecting an important package, you're often on
the lookout for the mail carrier. You peek out the window.
Listen for footsteps. Check the mailbox. When you pray, are
you on the lookout for God's answers? Not every answer will
be delivered when, where, and how you expect. So, keep your
eyes open and your heart expectant. Don't miss out on the
joy of catching a glimpse of God at work.

---

*Dear Lord, thank You for the reminder in the psalms that
You hear my voice. I am known by You and loved—so I can
wait patiently and be certain that You will answer in the
way that is best for me. What assurance! What peace!
In praise and thanksgiving, amen.*

THE UNEXPECTED

Jesus replied, "Why do you say 'if you can'?
Anything is possible for someone who has faith!"
MARK 9:23 CEV

What can we expect from God? The unexpected. Many people who came to Jesus asked to be healed. But how Jesus healed them was never the same. He put mud in a blind man's eyes. A bleeding woman merely touched His robe. Sometimes Jesus only spoke—and healing happened. Coming to God in faith means you can expect that He will act. He promises He'll respond to your prayers. How? Anticipate the unexpected.

Lord, I am so glad that You are a living, active God.
You're not a genie compelled to appear when the lamp
is rubbed; You're not a heavenly slot machine that spills
out answers at random. You are always listening,
always loving, and always answering. Amen.

AN ACT OF HEART

*Let love and faithfulness never leave you; bind them around
your neck, write them on the tablet of your heart.*

Dogs are known as "man's best friend." That's because dogs
are faithful. They don't hold a grudge or get so preoccupied
with their own lives they forget to greet you at the door. That
kind of loyalty comes easy to a dog. But for complex human
beings, it takes an act of will and heart. With God's help, you
can become a woman who others can depend on. Live out
your faith by becoming more faithful.

---

*Dear Lord, we long to be faithful as You are faithful—always
having the other person in mind and always working for
their good. Only Your Spirit can show us how to do
this and empower us—in our weakness—with Your
faithfulness. Be our guide and sustainer. Amen.*

PERFECTLY

Your kingdom is an everlasting kingdom, and your dominion endures through all generations. The LORD is trustworthy in all he promises and faithful in all he does.
PSALM 145:13 NIV

God's faithfulness to you never falters. It began before you were born and will last far beyond the day you die. Nothing you do, or don't do, can adversely affect His love and devotion. This kind of faithfulness can only come from God. Those who love you may promise they'll never let you down, but they're fallible. Just like you. Only God is perfect—and perfectly trustworthy. What He says, He does. Today, tomorrow, and always.

Dear Lord, forgive us for putting our trust in things other than You: in people, abilities, situations, money, habits, histories. All those things will fail us. Only You are the one true God, from everlasting to everlasting, faithful to every promise You have ever made. Amen.

SPiRiTUAL LEADER

A wise woman strengthens her family.
PROVERBS 14:1 NCV

Moms wear many hats. They're called to be chefs, teachers, maids, nurses, mediators, and activity directors—and sometimes all in the same 24-hour period. But God has entrusted you with an even more important role in your family. You're a spiritual leader. As you live out your faith, share the "whys" behind what you do. Point your children in directions that will lead them closer to God. A strong faith helps build a stronger family.

Father, it is a daunting task sometimes to shepherd the people entrusted to us. We long to "save" them and often think that our striving will ensure that. Forgive us. You alone can save. All we can do is point people to You. Help us to do so with grace and truth. Amen.

FORGED BY FAMILY

Our Lord, in all generations you have been our home.
PSALM 90:1 CEV

Your family's unique. You may be married, single, with kids or without. Parents, siblings, aunts, cousins. . .they're all part of the family God's placed you in. That family can be a testing ground for faith. That's because the more time you spend with people, the easier it is for them to rub you the wrong way—and vice versa. Consider what God wants to teach you through your family. Patience? Forgiveness? Grace? Don't put off until tomorrow what you could learn today.

Lord, we often forget to thank You: for our daily bread, for our homes and clothes and jobs, for our loved ones, for the breath that fills our lungs. Thank You also for the struggles we go through that You are using to conform us into the image of Christ. Amen.

INSIDE AND OUT

*God met me more than halfway, he freed me from my
anxious fears. Look at him; give him your warmest
smile. Never hide your feelings from him.*
PSALM 34:4–5 MSG

God knows you inside and out. He knows how you feel, right
here, right now. So why bother telling Him what's going on in
your heart? Because that's how relationships grow. Sharing
your personal struggles with a spouse or best friend is a sign of
intimacy. It demonstrates your faith in his or her love for you.
It also gives the other person an opportunity to offer comfort,
help, and hope. God desires that same opportunity in your life.

---

*Dear Father, we long to know You better; we long for the
intimacy that David describes in this psalm. And You long
for that too. You know every thought, desire, and struggle
already, but You long for us to run to You with
them—for our good and Your glory. Amen.*

CONTROL AND CLARITY

*But even if we don't feel at ease, God is greater
than our feelings, and he knows everything.*
1 JOHN 3:20 CEV

Do you regard your emotions as friend or foe? Your answer may
depend on how much they control your life. God created you
as a woman, an emotional being. Your wide range of emotions—
including empathy, anger, compassion, joy, sorrow, and fear—all
help you assess situations and decide on appropriate action. But
it takes God's wisdom to balance the power of your emotions.
When emotions run high, ask God for control and clarity
before you act.

*Lord, when I am ruled by emotion, I am not being ruled
by You. Forgive me for allowing my feelings and thoughts
to toss me like waves. I long to be ruled by You so that
my emotions become a rich source of praise
and a gift to share with others. Amen.*

GENEROUS

All the Lord's followers often met together,
and they shared everything they had.

ACTS 2:44 CEV

In our culture it's considered admirable to pull yourself up by your own bootstraps—or kitten heel pumps, as the case may be. But God asks His children to walk together, leaning on one another for support. Being generous in sharing our time, our resources, and our experience helps God's family grow stronger as a whole. As we hold on loosely to what we've been given, our arms will be more able to hold on tightly to those around us.

Dear Lord, we want to lift up empty arms to You. You alone can fill us. You alone can satisfy every desire of our hearts. And only when our arms are empty are they free to reach out to the lost with the life-giving gift of the gospel. Amen.

GOD'S FAMILY

May the God who gives endurance and encouragement
give you the same attitude of mind toward
each other that Christ Jesus had.

ROMANS 15:5 NIV

God's family is like your own biological family. You're bound to get along better with some members than with others. When God paints a picture of unity among His people, it doesn't mean disagreements and misunderstandings disappear. It simply means that the faith you share will encourage you to work through any problems that arise. Together, as God's family, you can learn what love really looks like, encouraging one another toward growth while helping smooth out each other's rough edges.

Dear God, today I pray for my church. It is so easy to be divided by small differences. Help us to live and love in unity and peace and walk in step with You. You are infinite, Lord; there is room at the foot of the Cross for everyone. Amen.

DOLLARS

*Remember the LORD your God, for it is he who
gives you the ability to produce wealth.*
DEUTERONOMY 8:18 NIV

A sense of entitlement comes with a paycheck. You earned it, so you get to choose how to spend it, right? But have you ever stopped to consider how the way God created you impacts your ability to earn a living? Take a moment right now to thank God for His part in your financial picture. Ask Him to give you wisdom, self-control, and a spirit of generosity as you choose how to use every dollar you receive.

---

*Lord, I have never wanted for anything. I have always been
fed, housed, clothed, and loved. Every time I have felt a lack
was really because I had turned away from You, away
from the joyful discipline of counting my blessings.
Right now, I recommit to giving thanks. Amen.*

JUST WHAT YOU NEED

"No one can serve two masters. . . .
You cannot serve both God and money."
MATTHEW 6:24 NIV

When you were a little girl, what was the "one thing" you wanted? You knew you'd truly be happy, if only it were yours. Adults often feel the same way. If only we had more money, this "one thing" could be ours! But when we focus on our wants, we become a slave to those longings. There's only "one thing" that truly satisfies—having faith in the God who loves you enough to provide exactly what you need.

Dear Lord, You provide for our every need. Thank You for being
a kind, just, loving, generous Father. Help us stop chasing
after things that only fill us for a moment; teach us instead,
to chase after You with all our hearts. You alone
satisfy us now and for eternity. Amen.

A TRUE PARADISE

If we confess our sins to God, he can always be trusted
to forgive us and take our sins away.
1 JOHN 1:9 CEV

Faith and forgiveness are two sides of the same coin. You cannot hold on to one without embracing the other. If you believe Jesus loves you so much that He would pay the penalty for your sins with His own life, then you must also believe that He wouldn't hold those sins against you any longer. If you're feeling guilty, talk to God. Your feelings are not always truth-tellers. God's forgiveness is what makes spending eternity with Him a true paradise.

Father, thank You for the size of Your forgiveness: as far as the east is from the west, as deep as the ocean, as wide as the sky. And You don't just forgive, but You take our sins away as though they had never been. Help us to rest and rejoice in Your undeserved mercy. Amen.

IMMEDIATELY. COMPLETELY. ETERNALLY.

*Be even-tempered, content with
second place, quick to forgive an offense.*
COLOSSIANS 3:12–13 MSG

When you put your faith in God, the very first thing He does is forgive you. He doesn't overlook what you've done. He forgives it. Immediately. Completely. Eternally. Choosing to follow His example isn't always easy. But it's always right. When others offend you, don't let your forgiveness hinge on their apology or repentance. You can wisely set boundaries and still offer forgiveness. Ask God to help you forgive before another's fault can fester into a painful, distracting grudge.

---

*Dear Lord, forgive me for the sins I hold against others.
Forgive me for the anger and lack of forgiveness in my heart.
Help me remember how much I have been forgiven and
extend that same grace to those who have hurt me.
Only Your Spirit can enable that in me. Amen.*

FREE TO BE

*I will walk in freedom, for I have devoted
myself to your commandments.*
PSALM 119:45 NLT

Without rules, what sounds like freedom can be chaos. Take driving, for instance. You need a license to operate a motor vehicle. That's not because the DMV is worried about your being a woman driver. It's because traffic flows "freer" when everyone knows and follows the rules. The same is true when living a life of faith. God's commandments help us build stronger relationships. We're freer to be ourselves—and love God and others well—when we follow His rules.

---

*Dear Lord, thank You that Your Word brings abundant life,
not restriction. Your fences bring us complete freedom within
the bounds of Your will. Your commandments were only
ever given for our good: to point us to the Savior,
Jesus Christ, who obeys perfectly. Amen.*

KEY TO FREEDOM

The Scriptures declare that we are all prisoners of sin,
so we receive God's promise of freedom only
by believing in Jesus Christ.
GALATIANS 3:22 NLT

Imagine being locked in prison for years. You're guilty, hopeless, and helpless. Then a beloved friend volunteers to take your place. You're set free as another woman takes your punishment as her own. How much do you value the cost of your freedom? In essence, this is what Christ did for you. When you place your faith in Him, you're handed the key to freedom. Honor Jesus' gift by living a life worthy of such sacrifice.

Lord, I would live differently if there actually was another
woman in jail in my place. I would continually tell of her
love and sacrifice for me. Her praises would always be
on my lips. You went to jail for me, Jesus! Whom the
Son sets free is free indeed. Amen.

ANEW

The faithful love of the LORD never ends!
His mercies never cease. Great is his faithfulness;
his mercies begin afresh each morning.
LAMENTATIONS 3:22–23 NLT

We all blow it. We let anger turn our words into weapons. We fall back into patterns we vowed we'd never repeat. We feel ashamed of ourselves as wives, mothers, or friends. But this is another minute, another morning, another chance to begin anew. Faith can break a cycle of regrettable yesterdays—if we let it. God offers forgiveness and a fresh start to all who ask. He never tires of us bringing our brokenness to Him.

Lord, when You designed the world to turn on its axis,
You gave us a picture of Your heart. Every day You paint
the sky with beauty; every day darkness turns to dawn.
We praise You for those reminders of how You bring light
out of darkness and beauty out of ashes. Amen.

AN INSIDE JOB

We look inside, and what we see is that anyone united
with the Messiah gets a fresh start, is created new.
The old life is gone; a new life burgeons!
2 CORINTHIANS 5:17 MSG

Faith is the ultimate makeover. But it doesn't hide who you are with a lift or tuck here and a fresh coat of foundation there. This makeover isn't external—it's eternal. And it's totally an inside job. Jesus referred to it as being "born again." Those old habits, regrets, and mistakes are behind you. Your past is forgiven and your future empowered by God's Spirit working through you. Let go of yesterday and grab hold of God's promise for today!

Dear Lord, thank You for this incredible truth. We are being made new—the old "us" has no power anymore. The Spirit that is in us now has immeasurably more power than the desires and fears that ruled us before we believed. We praise You, Lord, for fresh starts and new life. Amen.

MAKE TIME

Just as lotions and fragrance give sensual delight,
a sweet friendship refreshes the soul.
PROVERBS 27:9 MSG

Jesus' disciples were more than just apprentices learning the ins and outs of faith. They were also Jesus' closest friends. They walked together, talked together, ate together, and prayed together. When Jesus knew His time on earth was short, He turned to them for support. Follow Jesus' example. No matter how busy you get, make time for the friends God brings into your life. They may be God's answers to prayers you're praying today.

Lord, thank You for the friends You have put into my life.
Forgive me for often being too busy to make time to nurture
our relationships. My friends refresh my soul and draw
me closer to You. With them I get a glimpse into
the divine fellowship of eternity. Amen.

AUTHENTiC

Giving an honest answer is a sign of true friendship.
PROVERBS 24:26 CEV

Teenage girls are known for being petty and cliquish. But you're all grown up now. You're not only a woman. . .you're a woman of faith. That means it's time to put away childish habits, especially those that keep you from loving others well. A true friend doesn't play games or hide behind masks. She's honest about who she is, open about her strengths, weaknesses, hopes, and fears. Her honesty invites others to be as authentic with her as she is with them.

Lord, we long to be true friends, made not just for fair weather and easy answers but for stormy days and difficult words. Help me to be the kind of friend who is honest and speaks truth. Help me also to be able to hear truth and carry the weight of others' authenticity. Amen.

WHOLESOME AND EVERLASTING

*"I chose you. I appointed you to go and produce
lasting fruit, so that the Father will give you
whatever you ask for, using my name."*
JOHN 15:16 NLT

Pick up a banana at the supermarket, forget about it for a few days, and *voilà*! You wind up with a black, mushy mess. There's only one kind of fruit that doesn't spoil. That's spiritual fruit. Because of your faith in God, you can trust He's growing wholesome, everlasting fruit in you. You can nurture this fruit—helping it grow to maturity—by watering it frequently with God's words. Read the Bible, and then watch what God produces in your life.

---

*Dear Father, thank You for Your Word. It is the soil which
nourishes my faith, the light that strengthens my faith,
the water that renews me when I am dry and tired.
Forgive me for the times I have ignored Your life-
giving Word. Help me to dig deeply into it. Amen.*

PROPER CONDITIONS

The Holy Spirit produces this kind of fruit in our lives: love, joy, peace, patience, kindness, goodness, faithfulness, gentleness, and self-control. There is no law against these things!
GALATIANS 5:22–23 NLT

Fruit doesn't ripen through its own hard work. It doesn't will itself to grow juicier. Fruit just does what it was created to do. It grows into something beautiful and beneficial. God's Spirit is the only One who can bring this spiritual fruit to maturity in you. But you can provide the proper conditions to encourage growth. Have faith that God is at work. Put into practice what you learn. Then, have patience. Harvesttime is coming!

Dear Lord, thank You for promising to produce godly fruit in us through the work of Your Holy Spirit. Thank You for loving us so much and tending to us with such care. We long to produce the fruit that shows we have repented and are now followers of Jesus. Amen.

ONE STEP AT A TIME

*Because Jesus was raised from the dead, we've been
given a brand-new life and have everything to live for,
including a future in heaven—and the future starts now!*

1 PETER 1:3–4 MSG

The future isn't something that's waiting off in the distance.
It's right here, right now. Every breath you take brings you
into that future, one step at a time. And the future that awaits
you is good. Faith changes the course of your future as surely
as it changes the landscape of your heart. God is preparing
a home for you that will never be torn down, a place where
your questions will be answered and your longings, fulfilled.

---

*Lord, we long for heaven; we long to worship You as we were
created to do; we long for the close fellowship for which
we were intended; we long for perfect days without
end. Help us now to see heaven more clearly as well
as the blessings of these days on earth. Amen.*

WORTH WAITING FOR

"For I know the plans I have for you," declares the LORD,
"plans to prosper you and not to harm you,
plans to give you hope and a future."
JEREMIAH 29:11 NIV

For centuries, people have turned to fortunetellers, crystal balls, and horoscopes in the hope of glimpsing the future. Turning to anything, or anyone, other than God for this kind of information is futile as well as forbidden by scripture. It's also unnecessary. God holds our future in His hands. He has a plan and a purpose for what lies ahead. We may not know the details of all our tomorrows, but faith assures us it's well worth waiting for.

Dear Lord, You hold the past, the present, and the future
in Your mighty hands. You have known the end of the story
from before time began. Forgive us for trying to see past
You into the future. Help us learn to trust You
and rest in Your omniscience. Amen.

BiG-HEARTED

I am praying that you will put into action the generosity that comes from your faith as you understand and experience all the good things we have in Christ.

PHILEMON 1:6 NLT

When you choose to follow Christ, your faith opens the flood-gates of countless good gifts. You receive things like forgive-ness, salvation, a future home in heaven, and God's own Spirit living inside you. God's generosity is incomparable. It can also be motivational. When someone is incredibly generous with you, it inspires you to share more generously with others. Whether it's your time, your finances, your home—or things like forgiveness, grace, or love—follow God's example. Be big-hearted and open-handed.

Lord, sometimes I think I have nothing to give, but then I remember the gifts You have given me: forgiveness, salvation, hope. Those are incomparable riches that I have the privilege of sharing with others. They cost nothing, but they are more valuable than anything money could buy. Amen.

UTMOST LOVE AND CARE

*Have you ever come on anything quite like this extravagant
generosity of God, this deep, deep wisdom? It's way
over our heads. We'll never figure it out.*
ROMANS 11:33 MSG

Consider what it would be like to own everything. Absolutely
everything. Even the universe is under your control. In this
scenario, it seems like it would be easy to be generous. After
all, you have so much. But God treasures every speck of His
creation—especially His children. Entrusting us with free will
and with the job of caring for this planet was a risky venture.
Honor God's generosity by treating His gifts with the utmost
love and care.

*Lord, it's easy to be careless with things that aren't ours—
to trample, to litter, to waste. Help us see this beautiful
planet as a gift You've given us to steward as though it
belonged to us alone. And help us see other people
as gifts to nurture and protect as well. Amen.*

OF THE HEART

Let your gentleness be evident to all. The Lord is near.
PHILIPPIANS 4:5 NIV

Society honors a gentleman. By definition, he's someone who treats others with courtesy, thoughtfulness, and respect. In contrast, a gentlewoman is often pictured as a proverbial wallflower, soft-spoken, and easily pushed around. Gentleness is a characteristic of the heart—a trait God honors and exemplifies. You can be a spitfire with a voice like a foghorn who's not afraid to stand up for what's right and still exude gentleness. Allow God to help bring out the gentlewoman in you.

Lord, so often I haven't been gentle. I've been harsh, stern, and rough with others. I've been far from You in those moments. Forgive me. Help me show how near You are to me by the gentleness of my actions and words. Only Your Spirit living in me can do that. Amen.

GENTLE STRENGTH

*Always be prepared to give an answer to everyone who
asks you to give the reason for the hope that you have.
But do this with gentleness and respect.*
1 PETER 3:15 NIV

From surgery to tile painting, it takes a gentle hand to accomplish a delicate task. But sometimes gentleness is viewed as a sign of weakness. Gentleness is not less powerful or effective than strength. It's strength released in a controlled, appropriate measure. When sharing your faith, gentleness shows you care for others the way God does. Jesus was never pushy; He simply told the truth. Then He allowed others the freedom to choose what to do with it.

---

*Dear Lord, only Your Son was perfect in gentleness—because
He was also perfect in strength. Help me care for others in
the same way, speaking truth in love. Forgive me when
I fail, but help me keep sharing the hope that is
in me with gentleness and respect. Amen.*

LET GOODNESS FLOW

Whenever we have the opportunity, we should do good to everyone—especially to those in the family of faith.
GALATIANS 6:10 NLT

You can't be a good woman without doing good things. That isn't a rule; it's more of a reminder. Goodness flows naturally from a faith-filled heart. As you grow in your faith, you're changed from the inside out. You become more loving as you draw closer to our loving God. Your once prideful, self-centered heart begins to put others' needs before your own. Say *yes* to letting goodness flow freely from your life into the lives of others.

Lord, thank You that faith doesn't exist in a vacuum; it inhabits a world and sets in motion countless miracles. Help us look at our faith with clear eyes and see where it impacts others. Help us demonstrate our faith with good deeds done in Jesus' name. Amen.

GOOD MEALS

He satisfies the longing soul,
and fills the hungry soul with goodness.
PSALM 107:9 NKJV

When you're preparing a holiday meal, chances are you don't settle for "good enough." You rely on your favorite dishes, ones that look good, taste good, and are good for you. God feeds your soul similar spiritual fare. Like a good cook who consistently turns out good meals, our good God consistently bestows good gifts. Sometimes they're delectable delights; other times they're much needed vegetables. You can trust in God's goodness to serve up exactly what you need.

Lord, we don't always like what You serve us: chocolate cake,
yes; but celery, maybe not. Help us see that all the things
You give us are for our good, which makes them good,
regardless of their taste in the moment. When we
can't see what we need, You always can. Amen.

BY GRACE ALONE

God saved you by his grace when you believed.
And you can't take credit for this; it is a gift from God.
EPHESIANS 2:8 NLT

It's humbling to accept a favor from someone, especially when you know it's one you can never repay. But that's what grace is: a gift so big you don't deserve it and can never repay it. All God asks is a tiny, mustard seed–sized grain of faith in return. When you tell God, "I believe," His grace wipes away everything that once came between you and Him. Lies. Anger. Betrayal. Pride. Selfishness. They're history. . .by God's grace alone.

Dear Lord, we always feel like we have to do something to earn the grace we've been given: serve more, read the Bible more, witness more, pray more. But this verse reminds us that grace is a gift for which no repayment is necessary—or even possible. Thank You, Father! Amen.

UNFAILING LOVE

On the outside it often looks like things are falling apart
on us, on the inside, where God is making new life,
not a day goes by without his unfolding grace.
2 CORINTHIANS 4:16 MSG

When you first chose to believe in God, His grace wiped away every past digression you'd ever made from the life He designed for you to lead. But His grace doesn't stop there. Every day, it's at work. You may be God's daughter, but you're still growing. There will be times you'll stumble—times you'll look to yourself first instead of to God. God's grace continues to cleanse you and draw you closer to Him, reassuring you of His unfailing love.

Dear Father, give us Your eyes to see the new life unfolding
around us, even when it looks like things are falling apart.
If You are in us, You are at work in us. Help us look to You more
each day and follow closely behind You, walking in faith. Amen.

KEEP WALKING

Keep your eyes on Jesus, who both began and finished this race we're in. Study how he did it. Because he never lost sight of where he was headed.
<small>HEBREWS 12:2 MSG</small>

When following a trail, you're really following those who came before you. Physically, they're no longer present. But you can follow what they left behind. Maybe a marker points you in the proper direction. Perhaps you walk a path flattened by previous footfalls. Keep your eyes on Jesus the way you follow a trail. Read what other followers left behind—the Bible. Watch for signs of God's work in the world. Then keep walking, leaving a "faith" trail others can follow.

On this narrow path, Lord, sometimes it's hard to keep going. Our legs are tired, and we can't see the summit from where we are now. Help us keep walking in faith, reading the map of Your Word, and listening to the Spirit's leading. The view from the top will be worth it! Amen.

THE RiGHT DiRECTiON

*Each morning let me learn more about your
love because I trust you. I come to you in
prayer, asking for your guidance.*
PSALM 143:8 CEV

If you're navigating a road trip, just owning a map isn't going to get you to your destination. You need to compare where you are on the map with where you want to go, follow road signs, and evaluate your progress. God's Spirit works in much the same way. Each morning, ask Him to help you head in the right direction. Then, throughout the day, evaluate where you are and who you believe God wants you to be.

---

*Dear Lord, often I wake up in the morning and the first things
I think about are what's on my to-do list and how quickly
I can get to the coffeepot. Forgive me for thinking
of my own agenda and comfort and forgetting
You. I desire to put You first. Amen.*

SURPRISED BY HAPPINESS

*You will come to know God even better. His glorious
power will make you patient and strong enough
to endure anything, and you will be truly happy.*
COLOSSIANS 1:10–11 CEV

Faith is a journey. Like any journey, it's a mixed bag of experiences. You can celebrate grand vistas, then slog through bogs of mud—all in the same day. Though happiness is often dependent on circumstances, when your journey's guided by faith you can find yourself feeling happy at the most unexpected moments. Perhaps God brings a Bible verse to mind that encourages you. Maybe you see Him at work in a "coincidence." Where will God surprise you with happiness today?

---

*God, open up our eyes so that we can see Your mighty,
loving hand at work in our lives—from the smallest
coincidence to the biggest miracle. . .even in the
ho-hum days where nothing much seems to happen.
You are at work in every circumstance. Amen.*

MORE TO LOVE

Make me as happy as you did when
you saved me; make we want to obey!
PSALM 51:12 CEV

Relationships grow and change. If you're in a marriage relationship, recall that honeymoon phase. Loving each other seemed easy and exciting, pretty much all the time. Then comes everyday life. Apathy creeps in. The happiness you first felt may seem to fade. The same thing can happen with God. Don't settle for apathy when there's always more to love and discover about God (and people!). Ask God to help you look at those you love—including Him—with fresh eyes.

Lord, when I first married my husband, I longed to do things
that made him happy. I looked for ways to please him. Have I
ever been that way with You? Help me bring back the joy I had
when You first saved me, by seeking to please You. Amen.

SPIRITUAL HEALTH CARE

*The prayer offered in faith will make the sick
person well; the Lord will raise them up.*

JAMES 5:15 NIV

Prayer is God's spiritual healthcare plan. Modern medicine can do wonderful things to help a sick person get well. But God knows your body better than anyone. He designed it. He can heal it. Not every prayer for healing is answered in the way and time frame we hope for. Sometimes emotional or spiritual healing take place, while physical healing does not. God can raise us up in different ways. So call on Him. You never need an appointment.

---

*Lord, You know my every thought; You know my aches and
pains; You know my secret fears and sins. I lift them up
to You now—for renewing, for healing, for forgiveness.
You are the Great Physician, the Savior, the One
who makes all things new. Amen.*

SAFE IN HIS ARMS

My health may fail, and my spirit may grow weak, but God remains the strength of my heart; he is mine forever.
PSALM 73:26 NLT

Our bodies are miraculous works of art. But they don't last forever. When you're ill or in pain, God is near. As any parent who's ever loved a child knows, He aches with you as well as for you. When the hope of healing seems distant, if you've run out of words to pray, picture yourself safe in His arms. Wait quietly, expectantly. Listen for His words of comfort. Rest in His promised peace. Hold on to Him for strength.

Dear Lord, it is so hard to watch a child in pain and know that you cannot do anything for them except hold them, brush the hair off their hot foreheads, and pray. But You, Lord, are a Father who can heal, and You will— either now or in eternity. In praise, amen.

ANYTiME, ANYWHERE

Get up and pray for help all through the night. Pour out your feelings to the Lord, as you would pour water out of a jug.
LAMENTATIONS 2:19 CEV

There's probably no more common prayer than the word *help*. Even those who aren't aware they're calling out to the living God cry out for help in times of despair, fear, or pain. But you know God is near. You know He hears. In faith, you believe He will help. Regardless of your circumstance—big or small—don't wait until you come to the end of your rope to pray. Call out to Him anytime, anywhere.

Dear Lord, I'm calling out to You now. I am besieged by my sins, consumed by my worries, harassed by busyness. I need You to come into this storm, into my little sinking boat, and calm the seas. Help, Lord. I know You are answering; I know You are with me. Amen.

INViTE GOD

God is our refuge and strength, a very present help in trouble.
PSALM 46:1 NKJV

Real life doesn't resemble what's seen on TV. Problems aren't resolved in an hour's time. There may be seasons where you need God's help just to make it through today. . .and tomorrow and the day after that. During times like these, God's presence can be a place of rest and refuge. Go for a walk. Draw a bubble bath. Find a quiet spot to just sit. Then invite God to join you. Allow Him to refresh you with His love.

Dear Lord, we invite You to come. Our hearts are heavy with the struggles that fill our lives. We desperately need Your presence and peace. We need You to be our refuge and strength. Show us how to draw closer to You so that we may be refreshed by Your love. Amen.

MORE REASONS TO HOPE

Let us hold unswervingly to the hope we profess,
for he who promised is faithful.
HEBREWS 10:23 NIV

What do you hope for? *Really* hope for? Perhaps it's security, significance, or a relationship that will never let you down. Hopes like these are fulfilled solely through faith. Read God's track record as recorded in the Bible. He keeps His promises in areas like these time and again. It's true that it takes faith to place your hope in someone you can't see. But you're building your own track record with God. Day by day, you'll discover more reasons to hope in Him.

Lord, I need to know: is my hope really in You alone?
In my secret heart, am I holding on to something else as
my salvation? Search my heart, Lord; know my anxious
thoughts. And lead me in the way everlasting. . .which is
my only real hope in this life and the next. Amen.

HOPE OF HEAVEN

What you hope for is kept safe for you in heaven.
You first heard about this hope when you believed
the true message, which is the good news.
COLOSSIANS 1:5 CEV

Faith gives us many reasons for hope. A home in heaven is just one of them. But what exactly are you hoping for? The Bible tells us we'll receive a new body, one that never grows ill or old. Tears will be a thing of the past. We'll be in the company of angels, other believers, and God Himself. Scripture tells us words cannot fully describe what we'll find there. That's a hope worth holding on to.

Lord, we're likely to be surprised about a lot of things when we get to heaven. Questions of doctrine or theology will be subordinate to worship; we won't need to argue and guess anymore—we will know as we have always been known. Help us live now with that in mind. Amen.

WHO DO YOU SEE?

Do not think of yourself more highly than you ought,
but rather think of yourself with sober judgment,
in accordance with the faith God has
distributed to each of you.
ROMANS 12:3 NIV

A humble woman sees herself through God's eyes. She recognizes the unique strengths God has built into her character. She sees herself as a creative collage of personality traits, talents, and abilities. But she's also well aware of her weaknesses. She knows that without God, even her strengths would not be enough to catapult her into becoming the woman she wants to be. Look at yourself through God's eyes today. Who do you see?

Dear Lord, thank You for making me the woman I am, with my strengths, weaknesses, talents, inabilities, and quirks—both endearing and irritating. I am Yours, made by You and for Your glory. Help me see myself the only way I can see myself rightly—through Your eyes. Amen.

The Ultimate Gardener

*In simple humility, let our gardener, God, landscape you
with the Word, making a salvation-garden of your life.*
JAMES 1:21 MSG

Some women have a bona fide green thumb. They take a seemingly dead stick and nurture it into a verdant piece of paradise. Consider how ridiculous it would be for that once sickly stick to brag to his foliage friends about the great turnaround he'd accomplished in his own life. Obviously, all credit goes to the gardener. God is the ultimate Gardener. His focus is tending His children. Humbly allow Him to have His way in helping your faith grow.

---

*Dear Lord, thank You for the soil of faith in which You have
planted me and the life-giving water You shower upon me
when I read Your Word. I am humbled by Your tender care.
Help me to accept all You do—both pruning and
fertilizing—with thanksgiving. Amen.*

FULLY LIVE

I will be careful to live a blameless life. . . .
I will lead a life of integrity in my own home.
PSALM 101:2 NLT

One of the hardest places to consistently live out what you believe is in your own home. That's because those who know you best have seen you at your worst. Living a life of integrity 24-7 takes more than self-control. It takes a change of heart. Only God can transform a selfish, wayward ego into a woman worth emulating. Place your faith in God's power, put your pride on the line, and then fully live what you say you believe.

God, we are weak and can hardly go an hour without sinning in thought, word, or deed. Fill us, we pray, so that the Spirit in us would be from God, not from this world. We ask that You would shine brightly in our lives, so that others will see and praise You. Amen.

GOD'S WAY

In everything set them an example by doing what is good.
In your teaching show integrity, seriousness and
soundness of speech.
TITUS 2:7–8 NIV

It's said that *character* is who you are in the dark. If integrity is part of that character, you'll do the right thing whether someone's watching or not. It takes faith to remain morally upright, honest, and true to your word in a culture where it's considered acceptable to do the exact opposite in the name of getting ahead. But God's way is ultimately the wisest, most beneficial way. Through your integrity, God may teach others lessons they'll never forget.

Dear Lord, You know how I act when I think nobody is watching. You know the thoughts in my mind that I would never speak aloud. Forgive me for those hidden, secret sins. I long to be an example, even in the darkness, of what is good. Amen.

RESERVE OF JOY

*Though you have not seen him, you love him; and even
though you do not see him now, you believe in him
and are filled with an inexpressible and glorious joy.*
1 PETER 1:8 NIV

In the Declaration of Independence, American citizens are guaranteed the right to the "pursuit of happiness." That's probably because happiness is something that must constantly be pursued. Even if you catch it, you can't hold on to it. Joy, on the other hand, is a gift of dependence. The more you depend on God, the deeper your well of joy. Ask God to show you how to draw on that reserve of joy in any and every circumstance.

---

*Lord, forgive us for the days when we stomp around like
the weight of the world is on our shoulders, like everything
depends on us. That is a lie we tell ourselves when we forget
Your sovereignty. The weight of the world is on Your shoulders.
Everything depends on You. In praise, amen.*

UNLiKELY WAYS

*When troubles of any kind come your way, consider it
an opportunity for great joy. For you know that when your
faith is tested, your endurance has a chance to grow.*
JAMES 1:2–3 NLT

"Trouble" and "joy" may seem an unlikely pair, something akin
to sardines and chocolate syrup. But God seems to prefer the
unlikely. He chose a speech-impaired Moses as His spokesman
and simple fishermen as missionaries. These choices brought
challenges. But when faith is pushed to its limits, God works
in wonderfully unlikely ways. Regard troubles as opportunities
instead of obstacles. As you rely on God, His glory will shine
through you—and unexpected joy will be your reward.

---

*Dear Father, we don't welcome trouble and suffering;
we don't welcome the testing of our faith. Help us to reorient
our thinking to line up with Your Word. Help us consider
troubles as opportunities for joy and the growth of
our faith, which is worth more than gold. Amen.*

BENEVOLENT BALANCE

*What does the LORD require of you? To act justly
and to love mercy and to walk humbly with your God.*
MICAH 6:8 NIV

God is both merciful and just. His justice demands that restitution be made for the wrongs we've done. His mercy allows
those wrongs to be paid for in full when we put our faith in
Jesus' death and resurrection. One way of thanking God for
this benevolent balance is by treating others fairly, mercifully,
and with humility. When we "do the right thing," we love others the "right" way—a way that reflects our heavenly Father's
own character.

---

*Lord, forgive me for the times I have been short with
waitresses, cashiers, DMV employees, telemarketers,
and others. Show me how to act with mercy and humility
toward other people, even when they are not acting
the way I think they should. Only Your Spirit
living in me can accomplish that. Amen.*

ALWAYS RiGHT AND JuST

Be ready! Let the truth be like a belt around your waist,
and let God's justice protect you like armor.
EPHESIANS 6:14 CEV

A Roman soldier's belt was more than a fashion accessory. It held all his offensive weapons. A soldier's defensive gear included a helmet, breastplate, and shield—his armor. As a woman of faith, God is your armor. When you're under attack, God not only offers you protection; He promises you justice. Secure your life with God's truth. Then rest in the fact that He's working behind the scenes, always doing what is right and just.

Thank You, Lord, for the spiritual armor You have given us. Thank You for the helmet of faith, the sword of the Spirit, the breastplate of righteousness. In You we are strong and protected and have nothing to fear. Help us to face the enemy of our souls with confidence. Amen.

QUIET COMPASSION

You've had a taste of God. Now, like infants
at the breast, drink deep of God's pure kindness.
Then you'll grow up mature and whole in God.
1 PETER 2:2–3 MSG

Kindness is the quiet compassion that flows from a loving heart. It doesn't announce its actions with shouts of "Look at me! Look what I did!" It whispers ever so gently, "Look at you. You're so worthy of love. Caring for you is my pleasure, my delight." Being the focus of an almighty King's kindness can be incredibly humbling, as well as encouraging. Let both humility and joy foster gratitude—and growth—in you.

Father, don't let me be like a fussy baby—pushing away the hands that would soothe me and the milk that would fill my stomach. You offer that, Lord, and more. Help me grow up into the woman You created me to be by drinking deeply in prayer and the reading of Your Word. Amen.

WORDS AND ACTIONS

Everything depends on having faith in God, so that God's promise is assured by his great kindness.
ROMANS 4:16 CEV

A wise mother schools her children in the ways of kindness not only with her words, but through her actions. God works the same way. Through the words of the Bible, God encourages His children to treat each other with respect, generosity, and consideration. But it's God's personal kindnesses to you that encourage your faith. Today, consider the many ways God has been kind to you just this week. What will your response be?

Dear Lord, You have been so kind to me this week. You have fed, clothed, and housed me. You have kept me free from sickness. You have calmed my anxiety. You have given me fellowship with other believers and opportunities to praise Your name. You are so good! Amen.

PRiViLEGE

*If God has given you leadership ability,
take the responsibility seriously.*
ROMANS 12:8 NLT

It's a myth that lemmings will follow each other off a cliff. The same can't be said for people. Some people do unthinkable things as the result of following a leader who isn't worthy of admiration or imitation. If God places you in a position of leadership—whether at home, at work, at church, or in the community—recognize it for the privilege it is. Ask God to help you love those you lead, guiding them with humility and wisdom.

Dear Lord, thank You for the positions of leadership in which You have placed me. I ask that I would be a godly example of wisdom, humility, and generosity as I serve. I don't want people to follow me—in my own strength, I would lead them astray—but instead, You living in me. Amen.

A GODLY LEADER

Good leadership is a channel of water controlled by God;
he directs it to whatever ends he chooses.
PROVERBS 21:1 MSG

A good leader is a godly leader. She recognizes her strengths and uses them in a way that honors God and others. Most importantly, she recognizes her greatest asset is prayer. If you ask God for wisdom, He promises He'll give it to you. Whether you're leading executives in the boardroom or preschoolers through a lesson in sharing, ask God for the right words, right timing, and right attitude so you can wisely lead others in the right direction.

Dear Father, in the image of water, You give us a great picture of Your thirst-quenching, soul-restoring, life-saving, rock-etching power. We pray for Your wisdom to enable us to be vessels and channels for that power. Amen.

PRAY DAILY

*Start with GOD—the first step in
learning is bowing down to GOD.*
<small>PROVERBS 1:7 MSG</small>

Before you could read, letters were meaningless squiggles on the page. But with practice, and a parent's or teacher's help, one day everything clicked. Squiggles transformed into words—and stories. God is like those letters. However, you can't master the art of living by faith simply by studying about God. You need to humbly admit your wrongs. Accept God's forgiveness. Pray daily for growth and guidance. Then you'll learn who God really is and understand your part in His story.

---

*Lord, we gain freedom when we recognize that bowing to You
is the first step in spiritual growth. We are nothing on our own.
We have nothing without You. There is no place for pride
or perfectionism. Humble us, grow us, forgive us,
teach us, Lord. We long to be remade in You. Amen.*

EMPOWERED BY PRAYER

Everything in the Scriptures is God's Word. All of it is useful for teaching and helping people and for correcting them and showing them how to live.

2 Timothy 3:16 cev

Your brain is an amazing, God-given gift. It enables you to master new skills, solve complex problems, and mature in your understanding of life. In short, it enables you to learn. By reading the Bible, you learn how to grow in your faith. As you read, ask yourself, "What does this teach me about loving God and/or others?" Then apply what you learn to your daily life. Your brain, empowered by prayer, will teach you how.

Dear Lord, thank You for our amazing brains. Thank You even more for Your Word, which reveals Your mind to us. The Bible is the mind of God transcribed on paper. We ask for Your eyes and Spirit to prompt us to read and study it and to change us in the process. Amen.

INCREDIBLE POTENTIAL

As obedient children, let yourselves be pulled into a way of life shaped by God's life, a life energetic and blazing with holiness.

1 PETER 1:15 MSG

Your life has incredible potential. It's filled with opportunities to love, laugh, learn, and make a positive difference in this world. Faith turns every opportunity into an invitation: *Will you choose to live this moment in a way that honors God?* What you do with your life matters. But, ultimately, who you become is more important than what you accomplish. As your faith grows, your heart more resembles God's own. That's when you recognize where your true potential lies.

Lord, we have our own ideas about what our lives should look like and what we should accomplish. Give us faith to let our lives and goals be conformed to Yours. Help us see that we will lose nothing! Remind us daily that You will use people who give their lives wholly to You. Amen.

PART OF LIFE

Jesus said to her, "I am the resurrection and the life.
He who believes in Me, though he may die, he shall live."
JOHN 11:25 NKJV

Death is a part of life, at least on this earth. But because of Jesus, death is not something to be feared; it's a door leading from this life into the next. And faith is the key that opens that door. Whenever this life leaves you questioning, hurting, or longing for heaven, picture yourself holding that key. The more tightly you hold on to your faith, the more peace, hope, and joy you'll experience on this side of that door.

Lord, when I find myself fearing death—when my eyes
are focused on the here and now, and not on You and the
life to come—I ask that You would strengthen my faith
in Your promises. Help me fix my eyes on the
eternal joy set before me. Amen.

MAKE THE FiRST MOVE

God sets the lonely in families.
PSALM 68:6 NIV

In the beginning of the Bible, God says it isn't good for people to be alone. Then He introduces Adam to Eve. The rest is history. Family is God's idea—and it's a good one. Whether it's your own family, your brothers and sisters in faith, or a time-tested circle of familial friends, don't wait for others to reach out to you when you're feeling lonely. Make the first move. True love both gives and receives.

Dear Father, when we are feeling sad and lonely, send Your Spirit to comfort us and prompt us to reach out to others. Remind us of the family of believers surrounding us. Help us also to be a lifting, encouraging hand when we see others who are struggling. Amen.

NEVER ALONE

Jesus often withdrew to lonely places and prayed.
LUKE 5:16 NIV

Loneliness can make you feel like you're on a deserted island surrounded by a sea of people—yet no one notices you're there. But there is someone who notices. Someone who will never leave you. Someone who won't forget you or ignore you, no matter what you've done. You may be lonely, but you're never alone. Find a place of solace in the silence through prayer. Loneliness may be the perfect lifeline to draw you closer to God, the One whose love will never fail.

Lord, loneliness can turn us inward to gaze at ourselves and our problems, or it can turn us outward—to You. We ask for Your Spirit to continually remind us of Your presence and our need for You. If we love You, we are never truly alone. You are here. Amen.

ESSENCE OF LOVE

God is love.
1 JOHN 4:8 NIV

Burt Bacharach said it's what the world needs now. The Beatles told us it's all we need. Robert Palmer claimed it was addictive. Huey Lewis and the News talked about its power. What does God say about love? He says He's *it*, the essence of love itself. If, like the group Foreigner, you want to know what love is, look at Jesus. Everything He did, including sacrificing His own life, is what true love is all about.

Lord, there are so many songs about love. Yet, if love is divorced from You, it is temporary, imperfect, and powerless. You are the only source of true love. Help us to sing about Your amazing, sacrificial love and share that love with others. Your love will never disappoint. Amen.

LET LOVE SHINE

What if I had faith that moved mountains?
I would be nothing, unless I loved others.
1 CORINTHIANS 13:2 CEV

What mountain are you facing today? Perhaps it's the rec-
onciliation of a relationship. Or maybe it's just that pile of
laundry you've neglected. Whatever it is, it would be nice to
simply "pray it away." But faith isn't a gift God gives to make
life easier. Faith is God's classroom, in which we learn how to
become more loving—more like God Himself. Ask God to let
love shine through in everything you do—even sorting kids'
socks.

Dear Father, I ask for Your love to shine through in everything
I do—from the mundane chores of everyday life to the
once-in-a-lifetime moments. I can't muster up love;
it comes only from You. Holy Spirit, fill me so full
of love that it spills out to others. Amen.

FOCUS

A wife of noble character who can find?
She is worth far more than rubies.
PROVERBS 31:10 NIV

Some wives are more precious than royal jewels. Others are royal pains. How does your husband see you? As you grow in your faith, you may notice how everyone around you could use the lessons you're learning. But God asks you to be responsible only for your own growth. Focus on loving your spouse by praying for him, helping him, and encouraging him. Be the spouse you'd like to be married to and let God handle the rest.

Dear Lord, it's easier to look at other women and see how they are failing to be perfect wives. Forgive me for that critical spirit. Instead, Lord, help me be a blessing to my husband. Give me the humility to ask him how I could love him better—and then to change. Amen.

A THREE-LEGGED RACE

Marriage is not a place to "stand up for your rights."
Marriage is a decision to serve the other.
1 CORINTHIANS 7:4 MSG

Marriage is like a three-legged race. Unless you work together, you're likely to take a few tumbles before crossing the finish line. Think of faith as the rope that holds you close. It binds you together, whether you're currently in sync or not. As you communicate with God—and each other—God will help set your pace and direct your course. The more you allow God to humble your pride, the easier your relational race will be.

Lord, when we committed to our husbands at the altar,
we committed to a life of oneness. "Me" is no longer the
largest part of the equation. Forgive us for the selfishness
that makes us want our own way at the expense of
the other. Grow us in love and service. Amen.

AWARE OF THE DETAILS

*By faith we understand that the universe was formed
at God's command, so that what is seen was
not made out of what was visible.*
HEBREWS 11:3 NIV

It takes faith and science to appreciate the wonders of nature. Science describes the improbability of generations of butterflies migrating thousands of miles to specific destinations they've never experienced firsthand or the impossibly delicate balance of our orbiting solar system. Faith assures us God not only understands miracles like these but sets them in motion. Surely, a God who cares for the tiniest detail of nature is aware—and at work—in every detail of your life.

---

*Lord, when I look at the stars, I am reminded how small I am. . .
but also how much You love me. You didn't send Your Son to
die for the stars or butterflies; You sent Him to die for me.
I am of infinite value to You. Thank You, Lord. Amen.*

A WRITTEN INVITATION

Ever since the world was created, people have seen the earth and sky. Through everything God made, they can clearly see his invisible qualities—his eternal power and divine nature.
ROMANS 1:20 NLT

God's story is written in more places than the Bible. It's written in the glory of the setting sun, the faithfulness of the ocean tides, the symphony of a thunderstorm, and the detail of a dragonfly's wing. It's written in every cell of you. Take time to "read" more about who God is as described through His creation. Contemplate His organizational skills, creative genius, and love of diversity. Consider nature God's written invitation to worship and wonder.

Dear Lord, help us to be always pointing up—directing the gaze of others to You and Your amazing work in creation and salvation. But so often we are just pointing at ourselves. Please forgive us for our small vision, and instead tune our hearts to praise You. Amen.

HALF-BAKED?

Let patience have its perfect work,
that you may be perfect and complete, lacking nothing.
JAMES 1:4 NKJV

There's nothing delicious, delightful, or desirable about a half-baked cake. You have to wait until it's finished baking, no matter how hungry you are or how tight your time constraints may be. Impatience pushes us to take shortcuts and settle for second best. It can also rob us of opportunities to grow in our faith. The next time you feel impatience rising up in you, ask God, "What would You like me to learn while I wait?"

Dear Lord, forgive me for the impatience that wants to push people out of my way. I know You place roadblocks to slow me down and, in turn, cause me to grow. Thank You for unhurried drivers, for toddlers, for stubborn teenagers, for aches and pains. You want me to lack nothing. . .in sanctification. Amen.

ALWAYS HOPE

*Remember, our Lord's patience gives
people time to be saved.*
2 PETER 3:15 NLT

We're thankful for God's patience with us. He consistently honors us with time to grow, room to fail, and an endless supply of mercy and love. But we aren't the only ones who benefit from His patience; He extends it to everyone, including those we feel are slow learners or those we consider hopeless cases. In God's eyes, and in God's timing, there's always hope. Ask God to help you extend to others what He so graciously extends to you.

Dear Father, sometimes we think certain people will never be saved. We can't see Your sovereign plan from our vantage point here on earth, but we know You long for all to come to a saving knowledge of You. Give us patience to wait; You are working on those stony hearts. Amen.

PERMANENT PEACE

*Since we have been made right in God's sight by faith,
we have peace with God because of what Jesus
Christ our Lord has done for us.*
ROMANS 5:1 NLT

When world leaders sign a peace treaty, they pledge to keep the terms of an agreement. They aren't agreeing to like it—or each other. When you put your faith in Christ's sacrifice on your behalf, you make peace with God. God pledges to forgive your past grievances and even future mistakes. But the peace between you and God is more than an agreement. It's the rebirth of a relationship. This peace is permanent, based on unconditional love, not legality.

---

*Lord, when I put my trust in You, I stepped into Your loving hands. Now and forever, You are holding me. You promise never to put me down. And when You look at me, You see me through the blood of Jesus. . .as righteous.
Thank You for that amazing grace. Amen.*

A PERFECT COMPLEMENT

*"I am leaving you with a gift—peace of mind and heart.
And the peace I give is a gift the world cannot
give. So don't be troubled or afraid."*

JOHN 14:27 NLT

When attending a going away party, it's customary to give a gift to the one who's going away. Jesus turned this concept on its head, as He so often did with the status quo. At the Last Supper, the day before He died, Jesus gave all of His followers a gift—peace. When you choose to follow Jesus, you receive this gift. You'll find it fits your life perfectly, complementing any and every circumstance.

---

*Lord, You ask nothing for Yourself but our hearts—and You
give us everything else in return. Thank You for Your perfect
peace. It is our hope and comfort in this crazy world.
When worry and fear try to grab hold of us,
teach us how to cling to Your peace. Amen.*

A FRESH START

I have fought the good fight,
I have finished the race, I have kept the faith.
2 TIMOTHY 4:7 NKJV

Faith is more like a marathon than a leisurely jog through the park. During some legs of the race you'll be feeling strong and confident. During others, you may find yourself stumbling over questions, losing sight of the right path, or wanting to sit on the sidelines. To keep moving forward, run the race of faith one step at a time. Consider each day a fresh starting line. Moment by moment, with God's help, you will persevere.

Lord, I am so easily distracted by the cares of this world
and so ready to give up when things get hard. Forgive me.
Teach me to look at everything through the lens of
the Gospel and to preach it to myself daily. . .
then I will never lose my way. Amen.

LEAN ON HIM

Consider him who endured such opposition from sinners,
so that you will not grow weary and lose heart.
HEBREWS 12:3 NIV

Jesus literally went through hell for you. He suffered the pain of rejection and betrayal. He endured physical agony. He gave His life out of love for you. When you face what seems unendurable, hold on to Jesus. Cry out to Him for help and hope. Pray throughout the day, picturing Him by your side, holding you up when your own strength fails. Express your love for Him by leaning on Him. He's near to help you persevere.

Lord, when I imagine You by my side holding me up, that's not just wishful thinking; You are actually there. You promised Your disciples that You would always be with them, and that promise is for me too. Thank You, Lord. I am holding on to You. Amen.

"YES!"

We pray for God's power to help you do all the good things that you hope to do and that your faith makes you want to do.
2 THESSALONIANS 1:11 CEV

Faith gives you the desire—and power—to do things you may have never even dreamed of attempting before. Serving meals to the homeless. Leading a Bible study. Praying for an ailing coworker. Sharing your personal story aloud in church. Forgiving someone who's betrayed you. The more you grow in your faith, the more God will stretch your idea of who you are—and what you can do. Through God's power, you can confidently say, "Yes!" to doing anything He asks.

Dear Father, You give us the faith to step beyond what is comfortable and easy into a life of miraculous service. Please continue to strengthen us and increase our faith so that what we desire to do tomorrow is greater and better than what we desire to do today. Amen.

POWER SOURCE

We are like clay jars in which this treasure is stored.
The real power comes from God and not from us.
2 CORINTHIANS 4:7 CEV

What happens if your blow dryer won't blow? First, you check out the power source. Without power, a blow dryer may look useful, but it's really nothing more than a plastic knickknack. It's God's power working through you that allows you to accomplish more than you can on your own. Staying connected with God through prayer, obedience, reading the Bible, and loving others well will keep His power flowing freely into your life—and out into the world.

Lord, I long to be useful to You. In my pride, I think I can do things that will please You. Remind me that it is only Your Spirit working in me that can accomplish anything and that because of Jesus's sacrifice on the Cross, I already please You. In thanksgiving, amen.

OUT OF LOVE

If you are having trouble, you should pray.
And if you are feeling good, you should sing praises.
JAMES 5:13 CEV

If you're a mom, you know your children will ask for help more frequently than they'll express their thanks. You also know that much of what you do behind the scenes will never receive a word of praise. Of course, that's not why you do it. You do what you do out of love. The same is true of God. Why not take some time today to praise your heavenly Father for all the little ways He shows His love.

Dear Father, thank You today for the ways You show us love that would seem beneath Your notice: for songbirds, for blue skies, for a stone sparkling with mica, for crocuses, for the ability to whistle and skip! Help us to serve others in small, beautiful ways too, just like You do. Amen.

BECAUSE OF YOU

When your faith remains strong through many trials, it will bring you much praise and glory and honor on the day when Jesus Christ is revealed to the whole world.
1 PETER 1:7 NLT

The thought of God praising you may be a new one. But when Jesus returns, what you've done and overcome because of your faith will be visible to all. But it's not the accolades of others that make this worth anticipating. It's the chance to see God smile—and know it's because of you. In this life, you may feel your efforts go unnoticed. Rejoice in knowing God sees and praises everything you do because of your faith in Him.

These days are long, Lord. We know You are tarrying so that many more souls would be saved, but it is hard to wait. We pray that when You do come, we would be found faithful—working, serving, loving, proclaiming. We long to hear You say on that day, "Well done." Amen.

EASY TO RECOGNIZE

Be joyful in hope, patient in affliction, faithful in prayer.
ROMANS 12:12 NIV

How do you build a relationship with a friend? You spend time together. You talk about everything, openly sharing your hearts. Prayer is simply talking to your best Friend. True, it's harder to understand God's reply than it is to read a friend's text or access her phone message. But the more frequently you pray, the easier it is to recognize God's voice. So, keep talking; God's listening. With time, you'll learn how to listen in return.

---

*Dear Lord, I know You are listening, but I don't often feel it.
I long to know You intimately, but it's hard to continue
when I don't hear You answer back. Please help me
persevere in prayer, reaching out to You, who will
be there until my faith becomes sight. Amen.*

IN LINE WITH THE TRUTH

Everything you ask for in prayer will be yours,
if you only have faith.
MARK 11:24 CEV

Faith keeps our prayers in line with the truth behind what we say we believe. If we believe God loves us, believe Jesus is who He said He was, believe God has a plan for our lives, believe He's good, wise, and just—our prayers will reflect these beliefs. They'll be in line with God's will—with what God desires for our life. These are the kind of prayers God assures us He'll answer, in His time and His way.

Dear Father, we humbly acknowledge that the prayer offered in faith—the one You promise to answer—is the prayer offered in line with Your will. That means we might have to change what or how we are asking. Help us to remember who You are as we pray. Amen.

DRAW NEAR

I walk in the LORD's presence as I live here on earth!
PSALM 116:9 NLT

At times, God's presence is elusive. Although you believe in Him, you forget He's there. But He's like the air around you: invisible, yet essential to life. Remind yourself of God's presence each morning as soon as you awake. Breathe in and thank God for His gift of life. Then breathe out, asking Him to make you more aware of His hand at work in your life. Throughout the day, just breathe—drawing near to the One who gave you breath.

Most of the time, Lord, I wake up and immediately start thinking about my agenda for the upcoming day or some grievance from the day before. Forgive me. Your mercies are new every morning. Help me to rest—and rise— holding tightly to that promise. Amen.

ALWAYS WELCOME

*Because of Christ and our faith in him, we can now come
boldly and confidently into God's presence.*
EPHESIANS 3:12 NLT

Being in the presence of someone you've wronged isn't a comfortable place to be. Even after apologies have been offered and restitution made, a feeling of shame and unworthiness often lingers. This isn't the case in our relationship with God. When we set things straight through faith, all that lingers is God's love. Draw close to God in prayer. Never be afraid to enter His presence. You're always welcome, just as you are.

---

*Dear Lord, we can come before You boldly because You don't
forgive like people do. Our sins often stain and scar others
permanently. But You are holy, and Your forgiveness is as wide
and deep as the ocean; it erases our sin completely,
as though it had never been. Praise the Savior! Amen.*

GOD FIRST

"Seek the Kingdom of God above all else, and live righteously, and he will give you everything you need."

MATTHEW 6:33 NLT

Putting God first sounds like the right thing to do. But what does that look like in real life? Does it mean spending every moment reading the Bible or praying over questions like, "Paper or plastic?" Holding God's Kingdom as your top priority simply means that God's way becomes your way. Each day, ask God to help you live and love in a way that makes Him proud. Then, watch Him provide what you need to do what He asks.

Lord, when Jesus was on earth, He didn't have to think about putting You first. He knew You so intimately that Your will was His will. But He still drew aside from busyness, from the crowds, to pray. That is love. Teach me to seek You like that, Lord. Amen.

GOD'S PRIORITY FOR YOU

Honor Christ and put others first.
EPHESIANS 5:21 CEV

Eating, sleeping, working, praying, paying bills, staying fit, spending time with those you love. . .there are so many different priorities that cry out for your time each day. If you're struggling to figure out how to balance them all, allow your faith to help put things in perspective. What's God's priority for you? That you live a life of love and integrity. Keep these two things in mind as you decide what to add, and remove, from your schedule today.

Dear Lord, You determined the rotation of the earth in the beginning. This planet could have spun faster or slower, but You gave us precisely twenty-four hours. Thank You for that specific, purposeful amount of time. Help us use that time for Your glory. Amen.

SAVED AND SECURE

*You have faith in God, whose power will protect you
until the last day. Then he will save you, just as
he has always planned to do.*
1 PETER 1:5 CEV

Life can seem pretty precarious. The evening news fills our heads and hearts with stories of disaster and demise. In light of it all, our bodies appear so fragile. But the Bible tells us God has numbered our days. He's planned the day of our birth and the day we'll die. Nothing, and no one, can alter those plans. Like your future, your faith is under God's sovereign care. Within the power of His protection, you're saved and secure.

Dear Father, help me remember these verses when worry chips away at my faith. Help me turn up the volume of Your voice and Your promises until they drown out the voices of disaster and demise. You are in control. You hold us. We are saved and secure. Amen.

SHELTER FROM THE STORM

God's a safe-house for the battered, a sanctuary during
bad times. The moment you arrive, you relax;
you're never sorry you knocked.
PSALM 9:9–10 MSG

Your pumps are caked in mud. Your hair clings like a damp rag and you smell a bit like a wet schnauzer. But the rain doesn't let up. All you want is a warm, dry spot—a shelter from the storm. The Bible says you'll face all kinds of storms in this life. But God's your safe place, regardless of what's raging all around you. He's with you in every storm, offering protection and peace. Don't hesitate to draw near.

Lord, thank You for being our strong tower, our fortress in
times of war. We sure need that right now; the world gets
crazier with every passing day, and even the ground under
our feet is unstable. We are knocking, Lord. Thank You for
always being home to answer when we call. Amen.

FAR BEYOND THE BASICS

*God will generously provide all you need. Then you will
always have everything you need and plenty
left over to share with others.*
2 CORINTHIANS 9:8 NLT

Need is an easy word to use—and abuse. "I need new shoes to go with this outfit." "I need chocolate, right here, right now!" "I need some respect!" When God says He'll provide what we need, it's always on His terms, not ours. He provides everything we need to do everything He's asked us to do. Yet our loving God goes far beyond supplying the basics. He surprises us by filling to overflowing needs we never even knew we had.

---

*Lord, forgive me for complaining that You aren't listening if
You don't respond the way I think You should when I pray.
You're actually telling me I don't need what I've asked for.
You are God; You know exactly what I need and
what I don't. Help me rest in that. Amen.*

WHOLENESS

Jesus declared, "I am the bread of life. Whoever comes to me will never go hungry, and whoever believes in me will never be thirsty."

JOHN 6:35 NIV

When we talk about provision, our physical needs first come to mind: food, water, shelter, and the like. But we have spiritual needs that are just as essential as the air we breathe. We thirst for God's forgiveness and hunger for His love. Those who haven't yet put their faith in God often try filling this need with power, possessions, or relationships. But only a relationship with God can fill this void. Only faith provides wholeness to a broken world.

Lord, all we really need is salvation. If we die without it, we are lost for eternity; if we have it, then nothing in this life can shake our eternal security. It's Jesus; He's all we need. Thank You for providing all we need in this life and the next. Amen.

TRUE PURPOSE

*Now the purpose of the commandment is love from a pure
heart, from a good conscience, and from sincere faith.*

1 TIMOTHY 1:5 NKJV

"Did you do that on purpose?" Any mom who asks a child this question should be ready to carefully weigh the answer. But how about you? Consider what you've done this week. How much of it was truly "on purpose"? Faith provides a singular purpose for living: to love God and others. Fulfilling this purpose requires living prayerfully and with intention. Today, ask God to help slow you down. Consider your true purpose as you make your plans.

---

*Dear Lord, sometimes events—orchestrated by Your hand—
slow us down and we are stuck in a place we do not want to be.
Forgive us for not seeing barricades in an eternal light
and thanking You for them. We want to be where
You want us to be. Right here. Amen.*

SET iN STONE

*We humans keep brainstorming
options and plans, but GOD's purpose prevails.*
PROVERBS 19:21 MSG

When people mention "the best laid plans," they're usually bemoaning how the unexpected derailed what once seemed like a sure thing. God's the Master of the unexpected. That doesn't mean planning is a bad thing. It helps us use time, money, and resources in a more efficient way. But the only plans that are set in stone are God's own. Make sure your plans are in line with God's purposes. That's the wisest thing you can do to assure success.

Lord, we think we can say that a certain thing will happen at a certain time and in a certain way. We think our purposes will prevail. Thank You for the way You thwart those plans over and over again, so we learn—slowly and painfully—who is truly in control. Amen.

BEYOND YOUR COMFORT ZONE

*God wants us to have faith in his Son Jesus Christ and to love
each other. This is also what Jesus taught us to do.*

1 JOHN 3:23 CEV

People matter to God. All kinds of people. From celebrities to
"nobodies," pompous people to selfless servants, atheists to
those martyred for their faith. If people matter to God, they
should also matter to you. It's easy to only invest yourself in
relationships that feel comfortable and personally beneficial.
But faith sees beyond social circles and stereotypes. Ask God
to help you reach beyond your relational comfort zone. You
may be surprised by the gift of a friend for life.

---

*Lord, I want to see people with Your eyes. I judge by outside
appearances—attractiveness, eloquence, abilities—but it's
only when I try to look with Your eyes that I can see the
heart of people, which is where You are looking. Help me
look beyond the things that don't matter. Amen.*

TOWARD UNCONDITIONAL LOVE

You can develop a healthy, robust community that lives right with God and enjoy its results only if you do the hard work of getting along with each other.
JAMES 3:18 MSG

What are your greatest accomplishments? Earning a degree? Landing a big account? Lovingly leading a toddler through the terrible twos? Whatever you've accomplished, hard work undoubtedly played a part in your success. The same goes for relationships. Going beyond superficiality toward unconditional love is hard work. It's a relational journey that takes patience, perseverance, forgiveness, humility, and sacrifice. It's a journey God willingly took to build a relationship with you. Now it's your turn to follow in His relational footsteps.

Dear Father, nothing I do will matter if it is not done with love. No wisdom imparted with judgment will change anyone; no service done in anger will bless anyone. I am like a baby slowly learning how to walk like Jesus. Please hold my hand and guide me. Amen.

RESTART

You're my place of quiet retreat;
I wait for your Word to renew me.
PSALM 119:114 MSG

If your computer has a glitch, it's helpful to refresh the page or reboot the whole program by pushing RESTART. God helps us refresh, reboot, and restart by renewing us through His Spirit. When you're in need of refreshment—even if you've already spent time with God that day, reading the Bible, singing His praises, or praying—take time to sit quietly in God's presence. Push RESTART. Wait patiently, and expectantly, for a word from the One you love.

Lord, thank You that it is never too late to begin again.
It wasn't too late for the thief on the cross, and it isn't too
late for me today. Already, I need a do-over, and I ask for Your
Spirit to refresh me. I know You are eager to speak. Amen.

God Supplies

*Those who hope in the Lord will renew their
strength. They will soar on wings like eagles;
they will run and not grow weary.*
Isaiah 40:31 niv

Every woman has days when she's feeling weary. But sometimes, this feels more like the norm than just a down day. When this happens, welcome weariness as a messenger. It's a reminder you're in need of renewal. Get alone with God and ask, "Is there anything I need to change? What's out of my hands and in Yours' alone?" Allow God to do His job. Then, through the strength God supplies, do what you can with what you have.

---

*Lord, I am humbled that You care about my weariness.
Thank You for showing me, through it, that I am in
need of renewal. Give me the wisdom to know what
to change, delegate, or give up so that I can
live—close to You—in a state of rest. Amen.*

YOUR HEART

A kindhearted woman gains honor.
PROVERBS 11:16 NIV

Aretha Franklin sang about the importance of getting a little "R-E-S-P-E-C-T." But what's worthy of respect in God's eyes? In the corporate world, power and prestige usually herald respect. But God doesn't care about your title or notoriety. He cares about your heart, about how you treat others. Treating all who God loves with kindness is one way of respecting both them and God—and receiving a little "R-E-S-P-E-C-T" in return.

Dear Lord, I still find myself trying to gain respect through my accomplishments. Forgive me. Thank You for showing me that the only respect that matters is the respect that comes when others see the fruits of Your Spirit manifest in my life. Let that be my résumé and calling card. Amen.

ULTIMATE AUTHORITY FIGURE

Everything you were taught can be put into a few words:
Respect and obey God! This is what life is all about.
ECCLESIASTES 12:13 CEV

As a little girl, chances are you were taught to respect authority. Parents, teachers, police officers, the elderly—people whose relationship, experience, or profession put them in a position of influence over your life—were deemed worthy of honor and obedience. Now, as a woman of faith, you've accepted God as the ultimate authority figure over you. Don't let that title scare you. God's love tempers the power of His position. Respecting Him is just one more way of worshipping Him.

Lord, You are the Creator of the universe, and Your hand keeps it spinning in perfect motion. You are the Source of life and sent Your only Son to die for our sins so we could share in that life. Help us to grow in knowledge, respect, obedience, and worship. Amen.

HiS COMPANY

"Are you tired? Worn out? Burned out on religion?
Come to me. Get away with me and you'll recover
your life. I'll show you how to take a real rest."
MATTHEW 11:28–29 MSG

Faith is not a to-do list of assignments from God; it's an invitation to relationship. It's about getting to know who God is and who He created you to be. It's about resting in God's love and acceptance, not working harder to prove yourself worthy of His affection. If you're suffering from spiritual burnout, take time to simply relax in God's presence, enjoying His company the way He enjoys yours.

Dear Lord, we have a hard time resting in Jesus'
accomplishment on our behalf; we want to "deserve"
our salvation by doing something as well. Help us to rest,
rejoicing, in the finished work of Christ. We can add
nothing to it except praise and thanksgiving. Amen.

TiME TO REST

It is useless for you to work so hard from early morning
until late at night, anxiously working for food to
eat; for God gives rest to his loved ones.
PSALM 127:2 NLT

For three years, Jesus *devoted* his life to spreading the good news about God's love. This was an incredibly important job, one with eternal consequences. But even Jesus took time to rest. Although He dined with friends, taught, preached, and performed miracles, many times He left spiritually hungry crowds behind to spend time alone with His heavenly Father. You have many important roles to fill in this life. Rest is one of God's gifts that can empower you to accomplish what He's given you to do.

Lord, You know me. You know that I start every day with a
to-do list and how much pleasure I get in checking things
off. You know how "unproductive" activities irritate me.
But You give rest to Your loved ones. Thank You for
this timely reminder to stop. Amen.

DESIRED REWARD

It is impossible to please God without faith. Anyone who wants to come to him must believe that God exists and that he rewards those who sincerely seek him.

HEBREWS 11:6 NLT

Ultimately, it's not what you do, but what you believe that's rewarded by God. You can fill your life with good deeds, even to the point of sacrificing your life. But if your faith is in your own strength, abilities, or goodness—instead of God—your full reward will be the praise of those around you. However, if you're motivated by faith, the only reward you'll desire is pleasing God. Having faith in God truly is its own reward.

Dear Lord, we need a daily reminder that we can't please You without faith. Our good deeds do nothing to earn our salvation. They are only ever the fruit of our belief. Thank You that faith is enough to save us; thank You that faith also leads to action. Amen.

GOLD CROWNS

"The LORD rewards people who are faithful and live right."
1 SAMUEL 26:23 CEV

Exactly how God rewards His children is a bit of a mystery. The Bible tells us we'll receive gold crowns in heaven, which we'll promptly cast at Jesus' feet to honor Him. But the Bible also talks about rewards in this life. Our rewards may be delivered in tangible ways, such as through success or financial gain. But our reward may also be a more intangible treasure, such as contentment and joy. Treasures like these will never tarnish or grow old.

Lord, I ask You to fill my storehouse with the things that can never be stolen or destroyed. Love, joy, peace, patience, kindness, and self-control are rewards given by the Spirit—crowns that are a part of us and can never be taken away. Thank You for these imperishable rewards. Amen.

WiPED AWAy

God, in his grace, freely makes us right in his sight.
He did this through Christ Jesus when he freed
us from the penalty for our sins.
ROMANS 3:24 NLT

Saying you're righteous is the same as saying you're blameless. And that's what God says about you. Once you put your faith and trust in Jesus, every trace of your past rebellion against God is wiped away. It's as though you lived Jesus' life, morally perfect and wholly good. What's more, this righteousness covers your future as well as your past. Anytime you stumble, go straight to God. Confess what you've done. You can trust it's forgiven *and* forgotten.

Dear Father, we praise You for Your undeserved kindness to us and our undeserved righteousness through Jesus Christ. There is nothing we can say except thank You. There is nothing we can do except praise You for the forgiveness that covers our past and extends into our future. Amen.

THE LOVING CHOICE

*Pursue a righteous life—a life of wonder, faith, love,
steadiness, courtesy. Run hard and fast in the faith.*
1 TIMOTHY 6:11–12 MSG

Wearing white after Labor Day used to be considered taboo.
But what was accepted as "right" in your mother's generation
is not always considered "right" today. With God, the rules
never change. What's right is always right. Living a righteous life
means consistently choosing to do what's right in God's eyes.
Doing what's right may not always be the popular choice, but
it will always be the loving choice, the one God would make if
He were in your shoes.

---

*Lord, I am so swayed by other people's opinions, so afraid to
be different or to stand out from the crowd. But I know the
only opinion that really matters is Yours. Give me the
strength to stand for the truth. Give me the courage
to speak Your name to others. Amen.*

GOD'S FAVORITE GIFT

"Obedience is better than sacrifice, and submission
is better than offering the fat of rams."

1 SAMUEL 15:22 NLT

Suppose you had a daughter who broke every rule you made. She jumped on the furniture, hit her little brother, and swiped money from your wallet. Every day. But every evening, she offered you her dessert, telling you how much she loved you. The next day it was disobedience as usual. Have you ever been that little girl in God's eyes? Making sacrifices in God's name is commendable. But first, do what God asks. Obedience is God's favorite gift.

Dear Lord, often I don't see my own disobedience; I just
see the noble sacrifices I have made in Your name. Lord,
those sacrifices mean nothing if I expect them to cover
my sins. Only Your blood can do that. Only Your
Spirit can teach me obedience. Amen.

GLORIOUS BENEFITS

God sent Christ to be our sacrifice. Christ offered his life's blood, so that by faith in him we could come to God.
ROMANS 3:25 CEV

It's easy to focus solely on the glorious benefits of believing in God. Gifts like forgiveness, eternal life, a fresh start, and unconditional love are certainly worth celebrating. But each of these gifts comes at a very high cost. Jesus paid for them with His life. Jesus' sacrifice involved physical suffering, humiliation, betrayal, and separation from His Father. Choosing to follow Jesus will involve sacrifice on your part. Allow Him to show you how sacrifice can lead to something good.

Dear Lord, sometimes (or often, if we're being honest) we grumble about the suffering we are going through. Forgive us. Let us instead praise You for the suffering You allow us to experience. That is how, in Your inscrutable mercy, You are forming us into the likeness of Your Son. Amen.

FOUND

Salvation is not a reward for the good things
we have done, so none of us can boast about it.
EPHESIANS 2:9 NLT

You're lost at sea, drowning. There's no hope of saving your-self. Then, members of the Coast Guard appear. They pull you from the frigid water—no questions asked. They don't save you because of your impressive résumé or because you're such a kind woman. They save you because you need saving. Jesus saved you because you took hold of His hand in faith when He offered to pull you from the waves. Without Him, you were lost. Now, you're found—saved and secure.

Dear Lord, we can never do enough good things or obey
perfectly enough to deserve saving. Hallelujah! It is a free
gift offered to us when we recognize that we desperately
need to be saved. Thank You, Lord, for doing what
we could never do for ourselves. Amen.

NOTHING MORE. . .OR LESS!

"Jesus. . . There is salvation in no one else! God has given no other name under heaven by which we must be saved."
ACTS 4:11–12 NLT

God created you to live forever with Him. But like every other person since the dawn of time, you turned away from God to live life on your own terms. Yet God didn't give up on you. He sent His Son to pay the heavy price of your rebellion, to sacrifice His life for yours. When you place your faith in Jesus, you accept this gift. Your salvation's complete. There's nothing more or less you can do to be saved.

Lord, this is a gift that You are—even now—extending to everyone. It's not an exclusive club; it's not for the rich, or the poor, the beautiful or the very bad. It's for all who believe. Thank You for my salvation. Help me tell others about it with joy. Amen.

SECURE AND IMMOVABLE

I am sure that nothing can separate us from God's love—not life or death, not angels or spirits, not the present or the future.
ROMANS 8:38 CEV

You can feel secure in your relationship with God. God doesn't suffer from mood swings or bad hair days. He isn't swayed by popular opinion or influenced by what others have to say about you. God's love, His character, His gift of salvation, and every promise He's ever made to you stands firm, immovable. You can lean on Him in any and every circumstance, secure in the fact that He'll never let you down.

Dear Father, it is an immeasurable blessing to be loved in this way by You. I do not love like this. My love is fickle, forgetful, and frail. Forgive me. Help me to learn better how to love those around me by studying Your unfailing love. Spirit, love through me. Amen.

THE ULTIMATE BODYGUARD

Fear of the LORD leads to life,
bringing security and protection from harm.
PROVERBS 19:23 NLT

Fear sounds like a rather dubious route to take to find security. After all, you wouldn't hire a personal bodyguard you feared would harm you. But fearing God isn't the same as being afraid of Him. Fearing God means standing in awe of Him. After all, He's the almighty Creator, our sovereign Master, the righteous Judge of all. But this all-powerful God is *for* you. He's on your side, fighting on your behalf. Talk about the ultimate bodyguard!

If You are for us, Lord, who can be against us? Help us to remember these wonderful words of life when we start fearing things other than You. Nothing in this life—not death, not disease, not disaster—should overwhelm us. You are sovereign over everything. Amen.

ATTRACTIVE

Better to be patient than powerful;
better to have self-control than to conquer a city.
PROVERBS 16:32 NLT

Self-control is attractive to others and to God. That's because
self-control reflects God's own character. God doesn't act out a
whim. He waits for just the right time to do just the right thing.
Is there any area of your life where you wish you had more
self-control? God can help. Perhaps you need to lose weight,
just say no to gossip, or keep your temper in check. Ask God
for the desire and the discipline to wisely exercise restraint.

Lord, I need Your help in all those areas. Every day my tongue
gets me in trouble: it wants to speak too much; it wants to eat
too much. I pray that You would help me to hold my tongue
unless I am speaking words of praise or encouragement. Amen.

UNDER CONTROL

For the Spirit God gave us does not make us timid,
but gives us power, love and self-discipline.
2 TIMOTHY 1:7 NIV

Have you ever excused your own poor behavior by saying, "That's just the way I am"? God's Spirit tells a different story about who you are. Through faith, you have the ability to live a life characterized by discipline and self-control. But the choice to live that life is up to you. Consider the "character flaws" you see in your life. Ask God to help you get these areas under control, one thought, word, or action at a time.

Dear Lord, I blame others for my failures. I speak hastily
and without love. I judge without knowledge. I think of myself
first. I want to change these things about myself, and I know
that change can only come through Your Spirit.
Please, Lord, work in me. Amen.

THE BIG PICTURE

See how Abraham's faith and deeds worked together.
He proved that his faith was real by what he did.

JAMES 2:22 CEV

Abraham wholeheartedly believed in God's power and love.
So, when God told Abraham to sacrifice his long-awaited
son, Abraham prepared to do exactly what God had asked.
Surely Abraham had questions. He didn't know how everything
would turn out. In the end, God saved Isaac and commended
Abraham's faith. Serving God isn't always an easy path. You
may not see the big picture behind what you're asked to do.
But you can trust God's plan for you is good.

Dear Lord, Abraham said, when asked to sacrifice Isaac,
"God himself will provide the lamb." You provided then,
and You provide now. Jesus is that perfect Lamb, sacrificed for
our sins. And because You raised Your only Son from
the dead, we can trust You with our lives. Amen.

FAITH INTO ACTION

Offer your bodies to him as a living sacrifice, pure and pleasing. That's the most sensible way to serve God.
ROMANS 12:1 CEV

The most important choice you'll ever make is whether to serve God or yourself. The good news is that by choosing to serve God, you wind up doing what's best for yourself, as well. Caring for the body God's given you is one way of serving Him. That includes eating a healthy diet, exercising regularly, getting annual check-ups, and using your body in ways that honor God and others. It's just one more way of putting your faith into action.

Lord, thank You for the amazing body You have given me. Every morning I wake up and can see the sunlight, hear birds singing, and walk to the coffeepot! Not everyone is so blessed. Give me wisdom and discipline to take care of myself so I can serve You for many more years. Amen.

A FAVORITE LULLABY

I think about you before I go to sleep,
and my thoughts turn to you during the night.
PSALM 63:6 CEV

Sleep can be elusive, particularly during certain seasons of a woman's life. If 2 a.m. feedings, the throes of menopause, or simply mentally sorting through the demands of daily life are keeping you awake, set aside your frustration. Picture yourself pulling up the blanket of darkness, settling into the silence of night. Then turn your thoughts to God. Pour out your problems or lift up your praises. Ask God for refreshment and renewal. Allow God's voice to become your favorite lullaby.

Thank You, Lord, that when sleep is elusive, You are not.
You are right there beside us in the darkest, loneliest,
most anxious part of the night, ready to offer comfort,
conviction, and companionship. Our sleeping and rising
are in Your hands; teach us to rest in that. Amen.

SOUND SLEEP

The LORD is your protector,
and he won't go to sleep or let you stumble.
PSALM 121:3 CEV

For small children, bedtime can be a scary time. They may be afraid of the dark, of monsters lurking under their bed, or of bad dreams disturbing their slumber. Bedtime prayers can help calm their fears. They can calm yours as well. Knowing God never sleeps can help you sleep more soundly. If you're in the dark about a certain situation, if "monsters" are threatening your peace, take your concerns to God. It's never too late to call out to Him.

Lord, usually when it's bedtime, all I think about is how fast I can lay my head on my pillow and shut out the cares of the day. Forgive me for forgetting You. Help me, instead, remember to pause and turn my mind toward You in praise before I go to sleep. Amen.

A STORY TO TELL

It is with your heart that you believe and are justified,
and it is with your mouth that you profess
your faith and are saved.
ROMANS 10:10 NIV

For some people, faith is a very private part of their lives. But you have a story to tell that others need to hear. Sharing how God is at work in your life gives others permission to ask spiritual questions. Don't worry about not having all the answers. You can't. An infinite God will always be bigger than our finite minds can comprehend. But saying aloud what you believe is part of living and growing in your faith.

Dear Lord, I need Your help to grow in this area. I am so afraid
of what other people think of me and so worried about not
having all the answers. Forgive me for not trusting Your
Spirit to speak through me. Help me to start,
even in some small way, today. Amen.

THE POWER OF WORDS

Let everything you say be good and helpful, so that your words will be an encouragement to those who hear them.

EPHESIANS 4:29 NLT

Research tells us women speak about twice as many words as men do each day. That gives us twice as many reasons to pay attention to what we say! It's easy to let whatever pops into our heads pop out of our mouths, but the Bible reminds us that our words have power. We're responsible for how we use that power. Will we hurt or heal? Build up or tear down? Allow faith to help you choose wisely.

Lord, we want our children to learn to control their tongues, but so often we use our tongues without thinking. Forgive us for that hypocrisy. We pray that the words coming out of our mouths would be Your words. We pray for wisdom. We pray for the strength to remain silent. Amen.

BLOSSOMS

The godly will flourish like palm trees. . . . Even in old age they will still produce fruit; they will remain vital and green.
PSALM 92:12, 14 NLT

As you grow close to God, you blossom spiritually. But this is one flower that will never fade or fall. Your body will age, but spiritually you'll continue to grow stronger and more beautiful. The more time you spend with God, the more your character will begin to resemble His—and the more humble you'll find yourself in His presence. This is exactly the kind of woman God's looking for to do wonderful things in this world.

Dear Lord, You know how I have been struggling with aging lately. You know the aches and pains and limitations You've given me. Please help me to deal gracefully with them. But more importantly, help me to grow closer to You through them. I long for fruit that will last. Amen.

BEAUTIFUL THINGS

Do your best to improve your faith. You can do this by adding goodness, understanding, self-control, patience, devotion to God, concern for others, and love.
2 PETER 1:5–7 CEV

Only God can make a seed grow. But you can make conditions favorable to help that seed mature and bear fruit. The same is true with faith. Cultivate the seed of faith God's planted in you through obedience. When God reveals a weed budding in your character, pull it up by the roots. A fresh sprout of love? Water it regularly with kindness and sacrifice. Tend to your spiritual growth each day and beautiful things will begin to take root.

Lord, You long for us to grow and flourish. You aren't content to keep us small and weak in the faith. You send struggles—winds and droughts—that cause us to grow stronger and send our roots down deeper in You. Thank You for tending us with so much care. Amen.

STEP-BY-STEP

I can do everything through Christ,
who gives me strength.
PHILIPPIANS 4:13 NLT

Picture yourself in a race, struggling to reach the finish line. You're exhausted, discouraged, perhaps even injured. You're tempted to give up. Then a friend runs onto the course from the sidelines. She places her arm around your waist, inviting you to lean on her for strength and support. Together, step-by-step, you see the race to completion. God is that kind of friend. Whether the strength you need today is physical, emotional, or spiritual, God is there. Lean on Him.

Father, thank You for coming alongside me when I am weary. I feel Your comfort and strength flow into me as I meditate on Your Word, when I pray, and when I gather to speak of You with other believers. Thank You for meeting me right here in my weakness. Amen.

A SECOND WIND

*Strength is for service, not status. Each one of us needs
to look after the good of the people around us,
asking ourselves, "How can I help?"*
ROMANS 15:1 MSG

When you're feeling worn out, it's hard to think about meeting anyone's needs other than your own. But sometimes that's exactly what God asks you to do. Perhaps it's your children who need your help in the middle of the night. Or maybe it's a stranger whose car has broken down by the side of the road. When God nudges you to respond, call on Him for strength. His Spirit will rouse your compassion, providing you with a second wind.

---

*Lord, I am tired today, but I know You have put me in a place
where I can serve the needs of many. Help me to put aside how
I feel, to rely on Your strength, and to rejoice that You supply
my every need so I can meet the needs of others. Amen.*

IN LiNE WiTH GOD'S GOALS

Commit to the LORD whatever you do,
and he will establish your plans.

PROVERBS 16:3 NIV

Faith's definition of *success* differs from that of the world. Whereas our culture applauds people of fame, wealth, and power, faith regards those who live their lives according to God's purpose as successful. Committing whatever you do to God isn't asking Him to bless what you've already decided to do. It's inviting Him into the planning process. Make sure your dreams and goals are in line with God's. Then get to work—leaving the end result in His hands.

Thank You, Lord, that Your plans are to prosper me. But often I miss the most important part of that verse: it says Your plans. Not mine. In order to succeed, my plans need to be Your plans. Give me the wisdom to see where You are leading and the faith to follow. Amen.

CONSISTENT EFFORT

*"The market is flooded with surefire, easygoing formulas
for a successful life. . . . The way to life—to God!—is
vigorous and requires total attention."*
MATTHEW 7:13–14 MSG

Some people confuse luck with success. They want the reward of a successful life without having to put in the work. But success is something that's achieved over time. Whether it's in the workplace, parenting your children, or growing in your faith, success is the result of consistent effort toward reaching a goal. A successful life is made up of successful days—and a truly successful day is one that draws you closer to God and His plans for you.

*Dear Lord, when we think of a life where success is defined
in Your terms, we need think no further than Paul. He gave up
a high position as a Pharisee to be imprisoned, shipwrecked,
and reviled for following You. Give us the faith
to go and do likewise. Amen.*

GOD AT WORK

Give thanks in all circumstances;
for this is God's will for you in Christ Jesus.
1 THESSALONIANS 5:18 NIV

Faith gives you new eyes, along with a new heart. As you look more consistently in God's direction, you become aware of things you never noticed before. . .the miraculous detail of God's creation, the countless gifts He gives each day, His answers to prayer, and His persistence in bringing something positive out of even the most negative circumstances. It's good to notice God at work. It's even better to say "thank You" when you do. What will you thank Him for today?

Lord, I thank You for the view outside my window, for the
warm clothes I am wearing, for the smell of pancakes from
the kitchen, for the voices of my children and husband,
for the clink of forks on plates. You are present in
this house this morning, and I praise You. Amen.

SPECiAL PEOPLE

I have not stopped giving thanks for you,
remembering you in my prayers.
Ephesians 1:16 niv

There are many ways of showing gratitude. You can send flowers or share a hug. You can say "thanks" with a note, text, e-mail, or phone call. But have you ever considered expressing your gratitude via prayer? Asking for God's guidance and blessing on those who've generously touched your life with their love takes thankfulness to the next level—an eternal one. It also reminds you to thank God for His gift of bringing these special people into your life.

Dear Father, remind me when my mind wanders to unprofitable
places that I need to pray instead. Bring people to my mind
who have touched my life in eternal ways. Thankfulness brings
me joy and reminds me how You have been faithful
to me through other believers. Amen.

CHANGED MINDS

Create pure thoughts in me and make me faithful again.
PSALM 51:10 CEV

Living a life that pleases God is more than doing the right thing. It's also thinking the right thing. That's because faith isn't about appearances. It's about reality. It's about all of you: body, mind, and spirit. This transformation doesn't happen overnight. But the more time you spend with God, the more aware you'll become of random thoughts that don't line up with your faith. Take those thoughts to God. Ask Him to help change your mind for good.

Lord, we put on a good face when behind that smiling mask lurk thoughts too wicked, despair too deep, to say aloud. We long to be transformed. Discipline us for the long work of sanctification. You are in the business of changing sinners from the inside out. Amen.

FLiP THE SWiTCH

Keep your minds on whatever is true, pure, right, holy,
friendly, and proper. Don't ever stop thinking about
what is truly worthwhile and worthy of praise.

PHILIPPIANS 4:8 CEV

Some trains of thought need to be derailed. That's because they don't lead you closer to becoming the woman God created you to be. But like a switch operator who changes the track a train is on to save it from disaster, you can change the direction of your thoughts. If others could read your mind and you'd be embarrassed by what they read, flip the switch. Choose to focus on something worthy of your time and God's praise.

Dear Lord, when my mind leads me astray, give me the
strength to turn to scripture instead. Help me today—
and tomorrow and in the days to come—to fill my thoughts
with Your Word so that it is what I meditate
upon in unoccupied moments. Amen.

WHAT LiES AHEAD

The word of the LORD holds true,
and we can trust everything he does.
PSALM 33:4 NLT

You confide in a friend, because she's proven herself faithful over time. She won't lie. What she says she'll do, she does. You trust in her love, because you believe she has your best interests at heart. God is this kind of friend. It takes time to build your own track record of trust with Him. As you do, consider His faithfulness to those in the Bible. God's past faithfulness can help you trust Him for whatever lies ahead.

Lord, it's probably a good thing that we can't see the future.
Instead, like children clinging to the protective hands of
a father, we hold fast to the One who holds the future.
You will never fail us. What we do know is that
You are faithful and will prevail. Amen.

THE LiTTLE AND BiG THiNGS

Trust in the LORD with all your heart,
and lean not on your own understanding.
PROVERBS 3:5 NKJV

If you lean against a wall, you have faith in its integrity. You trust it won't crumble and leave you in a heap on the floor. If you trust God, you'll lean on Him. This is more than saying, "I believe." This is living what you believe. You may not always understand the "whys" behind God's ways, but the more you risk trusting Him with the little things, the more confident you'll be entrusting Him with the big ones.

Dear Lord, the longer I know You, the more I trust that what You say will come to pass. Thank You for increasing my faith through the blessings and trials You have allowed in my life. You are my strong tower, my Rock, my steady anchor. You will hold me fast. Amen.

TRUST THE TRUTH

Jesus answered, "I am the way and the truth and the life. No one comes to the Father except through me."

JOHN 14:6 NIV

Believing all good people go to heaven sounds nice. But it doesn't make sense. How do you measure goodness? Where's the cutoff between being "in" and being "out"? Spiritual truths cannot be relative or change according to how we feel. It must be timeless, steadfast—like Jesus. Jesus said that putting our faith in Him is the only way we can be reconciled with God and receive eternal life. Trust the truth. Trust Jesus.

Lord, it seems too simple. We want to do something to earn our salvation. But praise God, Jesus did it all on the Cross, and we don't need to—and actually can't—add anything to that. Help us rest and rejoice in the finished work of Christ. Amen.

WHOLLY TRUE

Lead blameless lives and do what is right,
speaking the truth from sincere hearts.
PSALM 15:2 NLT

The truth can't be twisted or stretched. It can't masquerade as a "half" truth or a "little white lie." If what you say isn't wholly true, it isn't the truth. Period. Speaking the truth doesn't mean saying aloud every thought that enters your head. It means passing out words like gifts. Choose each one carefully. Then wrap it in love and respect. Be as honest and truthful with others as God has been with you.

Dear Father, a lie contaminates everything it touches.
Forgive me for the times I have "shaded" the truth or spoken
outright falsehoods. I long to speak the truth from a sincere
heart, as Your Word commands. Only Your Spirit
living in me can help me do that. Amen.

THE PERFECT HARVEST

The LORD longs to be gracious to you; therefore he will rise up to show you compassion. For the LORD is a God of justice. Blessed are all who wait for him!
ISAIAH 30:18 NIV

God is the Master of perfect timing because He can see straight across the grand scheme of history. He can tell if what you're waiting for today would be even better if it was received tomorrow—or years down the road. As you grow in your faith, you'll grow to trust God's timing more and more. Expect Him to surprise you with the perfect harvest always delivered at exactly the right time.

Lord, You see the end from the beginning. From the vantage point of heaven, our stories are already told, finished in surprising and glorious ways. Help us trust that what Your hands have written will be just what we need and desire most. In love and faith, amen.